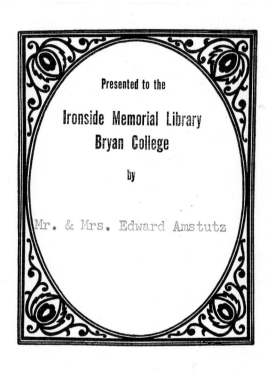

Administering
Church Training

PHILIP B. HARRIS
AND STAFF

CHURCH TRAINING DEPARTMENT
BAPTIST SUNDAY SCHOOL BOARD

Convention Press
NASHVILLE   TENNESSEE

Code Number: Church Study Course
This book is course number 6402 of subject area 64
in The New Church Study Course
Library of Congress Catalog Card Number: 71-88062
Printed in the United States of America
25. JUL 69 R.R.D.

Contents

Contents

Foreword

THE GROWTH of organized training in the Southern Baptist Convention has been phenomenal. The program of training in a church has developed like a romance to Southern Baptist life. The present training program is a backward glance with profound gratitude and a forward look with keen anticipation.

In 1916, 20 percent of the churches reported Baptist Young People's Unions. In 1929, more than 50 percent of the churches had organized Baptist Young People's work. In 1934, the name of the training program was changed to the Baptist Training Union. In 1969, 82 percent of the churches had organized Baptist Training Union work.

Church members have always needed training but never before has the challenge to train been so great. Trained, committed church members are needed to communicate the gospel to today's world.

The spirit of the age is a quest for something better than life as it has been. The search for meaning in life and for vitality in religion is intense. If churches are to fulfil their mission in this age, members and leaders must be trained. A new attitude toward training and a deeper commitment to training in a church must be instilled in the hearts of church leaders and church members.

The following tasks have been identified as making up the training program of a church:

1. Orient new church members
2. Train church members to perform the functions of a church
3. Train church leaders
4. Teach Christian theology, Christian ethics, Christian history, and church polity and organization
5. Provide and interpret information regarding the work of the church and denomination

This statement of tasks clarifies and sharpens areas of work which have been a part of Training Union in the past. In addition, it broadens the responsibility of the church training program, especially in areas of new church member orientation and church leader training.

The church training program has no reason for being, except to meet the training needs of church members. It is a quest for commitment, a quest for involvement, and a quest for effectiveness in the life and work of a church.

Those who serve their churches in the space age through the church training program face a tremendous challenge. It is the challenge to rise above a "business as usual" attitude toward training. In every realm about us—in business, in education, in professional circles—training is a must. It is an imperative; not only for growth and progress, but for survival itself.

It takes trained church members to spread the good news of Christ in an increasingly sophisticated and unreceptive world. Both the Scriptures and reason answer that church members must grow in knowledge, understanding, and skill. What responses will the churches make in the seventies? Surely we will answer with a renewed commitment to the imperative of training for the work of Christian service!

The author is indebted to many persons for contributions made in developing ADMINISTERING CHURCH TRAINING.

Personnel of the Church Training Department of the Sunday School Board have contributed liberally of their time and creative abilities in the writing of this book. These persons include: Raymond Rigdon, Harvey T. Gibson, Jimmy P. Crowe, Versil Crenshaw, Forrest Watkins, and Donald Trotter who served as editorial coordinator.

Church Training Department secretaries in the various states of the Southern Baptist Convention also made valuable contributions to the development of the manuscript.

Acknowledgement is made of the tremendous contributions made by other staff members, editors, and consultants of the Church Training Department and to Mrs. Idus V. Owensby who turned manuscript copy into printable book form.

PHILIP B. HARRIS

EDITOR'S NOTE: The name "Training Union" is used interchangeably with descriptive terms such as "church training" and "church training program." For example, the Training Union council is the same as the church training council. The Training Union director is the same as the director of church training.

ADMINISTERING CHURCH TRAINING

Chapter One

QUEST
FOR ESSENTIAL TRAINING

WE ARE LIVING in a time of rapid change. In the lifetime of many church training leaders, the daily routine of members of our churches has moved from relatively simple activities of the horse-and-buggy days to highly complex transactions in a computerized space age.

Technological and cultural changes have brought into focus many new problems. How do the doctrinal beliefs preached in brush arbors a few decades ago apply in our present electronic age? How can the love of God be communicated to highly educated persons? Are the moral standards advocated to young people in the old BYPU days realistic for youth now in church training? After all, is morality simply a matter of applying Christian love in specific problems of morality? How can the church make a significant impact on our highly secularized society?

If our churches are to continue to exist as effective forces for Christ, we must deal realistically with contemporary problems. One of their best ways to deal with such problems is to train growing Christians to work together in a vital Christian fellowship and to live and witness daily as responsible Christian disciples.

This challenging task calls for a new training program in our churches. Many old approaches were good and should be continued. Other approaches need to be replaced by ones more suited to the needs and conditions of our present day.

THE NATURE OF TRAINING

The urgency for training church members calls for a clear understanding of what training is. Training, as used here, is the educational process designed to improve individual or group performance. Training is not simply studying about something. Training is a cultivation of understandings, attitudes, and skills necessary to achieve. Training enhances proficiency and requires practice. As David R. Hunter said, "If our objective is to help people confront and react to the deepest process that is at work both in their soul and in their life as a society, then the concept of training has a degree of activity, of ongoing aliveness." [1]

Training to improve performance may be either specific or general. Much of church training is designed to develop in persons the ability to deal with specific situations. Two examples of specific training in Christian education are: (1) parents learning to recognize the learning readiness of their children, and effectively guiding their growth; and (2) college students becoming sensitive to the attitudes, understandings, and religious frames of reference of unsaved friends in order to more effectively witness to them.

Not all training is designed to develop abilities to perform in specific types of life situations. Life is too complicated and society is changing too rapidly for a church to expect to provide members with special training for every specific situation they may face. Much of the training process needs to be designed to improve general church member competence. Government military academies provide broad curriculums designed to train competent military leaders. Likewise, a church must train its members to be resourceful in dealing with unanticipated problems and situations.

---

1. David R. Hunter, *Christian Education as Engagement*. Published by the Seabury Press, Inc., New York. © 1963 by the Trustees of the Lester Bradner Fund, p. 50.

A sound training program places strong emphasis on helping us to *be* as well as to *do*. In Christian education, we must be trained in how to *be* true Christian disciples. Only as we grow as disciples can we be trained to *do* the things which we as Christians should do.

This emphasis on general training does not overshadow the need for specific training for particular situations. Both are important, and each must have its rightful place in a good program of training.

The church training program gives appropriate attention to three personal factors directly related to improved performance. These factors are understandings, attitudes, and skills.

Certain basic knowledge and understandings are essential to improved performance. An architect must understand materials and design to succeed in his trade. The more complex the performance for which training is being offered, the broader the base of knowledge and understanding must be. Some soul-winning efforts have engendered antagonism because the would-be soul-winner has memorized Bible passages, but he does not understand, or is insensitive to, the condition of the lost person or the nature and significance of the conversion experience.

The cultivation of right attitudes is an important element in training. Persons may have the knowledge and skill required for effective performance, yet lack the proper attitude toward their work or toward fellow workers.

Skill development is a third phase of training. All of the emphasis on understandings and attitudes is related to improved performance, in being able to live and witness more effectively in contemporary society.

TYPES OF TRAINING

The church training program builds on and improves the types of training which have characterized Training Union work during recent years. These are: the orientation of new church members, the training of church members and their children, and the training of leaders. In this book are chapters dealing with each of these types of training. Our purpose now is to gain an overview of the training provided by the church training program.

1. New Church Member Orientation

All persons received into the fellowship of a church have a special training need. New converts need basic training in the Christian faith and in the life and work of the church. New member orientation is a vital link tying the church's evangelistic thrust to win the lost to its educational efforts to help church members become mature and effective Christians. New members who transfer from other Baptist churches need an introduction into the life and work of the church they have joined. When new members come from a church of another denomination, their need for new member orientation may be even greater.

(1) HOW SHOULD THE ORIENTATION BE SCHEDULED?

Orientation for new church members is provided through counseling, instruction, and activities aimed at involving new members in the life of the church. Counseling is best done on an individual basis, but it may be done in a group. The choice of approach depends upon such factors as:

- The number of persons to be trained
- The suitability of schedule to individual's needs
- The availability of capable instructors
- The ratio of new converts to transfers
- The availability of suitable space

Although the basic intent of new church member orientation is the same for all members, the approach must be flexible enough to meet the distinctive needs of new converts and members who transfer from other Baptist churches. Sunday evening is a prime time for new member orientation, but it may be offered at any time convenient to the members.

(2) WHAT TRAINING IS OFFERED?

The purpose of counseling sessions with converts is to help them to better understand the meaning of their conversion and their church membership. New converts may have special problems which will require individual attention. The person leading the counseling should be aware of spiritual problems of the convert and assist him in finding answers to his problems. In addition, the leader should lead the convert to feel that he is essential to the church and that the church is interested in helping him mature as a Christian.

Two counseling sessions for new converts are suggested. These would deal with:

- The meaning of conversion
- The meaning of church membership

New members who are transferring from another Baptist church may be asked to share their testimony of conversion.

Ten topics are recommended for consideration in the instructional sessions with converts. They are:

- Your New Life in Christ
- Your Growth as a Christian
- Your Bible and Its Use
- Your Church and Its Covenant
- Your Church and Its Beliefs
- Your Church Working Together
- Your Church Working with Others
- Your Church and Its History
- Your Church and Your Home
- Sharing Your Faith

For new church members who are transferring from another Baptist church, five topics *may be* sufficient as a minimum. They are:

- Your Church and Its Covenant
- Your Church and Its Beliefs
- Your Church Working Together
- Your Church Working with Others
- Your Church and Its History

Each transfer member may be invited to attend the additional sessions for new converts if he feels they will be of value to him.

A summary session is extremely important both for converts and transfers. It consists of a review of the instructional sessions with opportunity for participants to raise additional questions. In this review session, there should also be a strong emphasis on enlistment into the regular program organizations.

2. Church Member Training

There was a time when training was considered to be only for children and youth. It was assumed that when one became an adult, he quit learning.

With rapid changes taking place in our society, training has become essential for persons of all ages.

A prominent professional leader told a group of his colleagues that their training, if more than five years old, might be a liability to them. Their profession had changed so drastically, that leaders in the field must be in continual training to keep current. The alternative, he warned, was frustration, failure, and oblivion.

Present-day Christians must continue in training if they are to live as meaningful and effective disciples. With the drastic changes taking place in society, training for Christian living and service must be a lifelong activity.

In order to train its members, a church must analyze its training needs periodically.

(1) WHAT KIND OF TRAINING IS OFFERED?

Four broad areas of training are included in the church training curriculum. These are: Christian theology, Christian ethics, Christian history, and church polity and organization. Each of these areas has special significance in present-day life.

Christian theology is concerned with the great realities of the Christian faith. Broad areas include God, man, sin and Satan, salvation, the church, the Bible, and last things. The emphasis in the church training program is not only on understanding these basic doctrines but also in experiencing these doctrines as dynamic realities, learning to express one's beliefs effectively, and living daily in the light of these spiritual realities. For example, a unit on the priesthood of believers might contain learning activities designed to help persons discover practical ways to reflect in their everyday lives this great doctrine of the Christian faith. Another Christian theology unit might begin with practical problems in interpersonal relationships and stimulate persons to discover Christian doctrines which apply to these problems.

Another curriculum area is Christian ethics. Christian ethics is concerned with God's ideals for living. These ideals are set forth in the Scriptures and thus provide the "oughtness" of the Christian life. Training in Christian ethics includes in part, exploration of basic principles and norms, personal ethics, interpersonal relationships, relationships of groups, intergroup relations, family living, Christian citizenship, daily work, and the economic life. Age-group units are designed to help members of the church training program to function as effective Christians in each of these areas.

Christian history is another of the curriculum areas. The emphasis here is not on the facts of history, but a search for historical insights which help us deal more constructively with the problems of life.

Church polity and organization is the fourth curriculum area. If members of the church training program are to work effectively through their churches, they need to understand why and how a Baptist church does its work. Informed members are more likely to be motivated to be good stewards of their time, talents, and money in fulfilling the church's mission.

(2) HOW ARE TRAINING UNITS RELATED?

The church training program provides church members and their children with opportunities for training throughout life in these broad curriculum areas. The training on each level is geared to the interests and life needs of persons of that age level. For example, on the preschool level, training in Christian theology is expressed in activities which help young children develop feelings such as the feeling that God loves them and that the church is a place where God's people worship, learn, and work together.

Although the church training curriculum areas are expressed in the preschool curriculum, these areas are not always directly identifiable as such. The preschool curriculums for all program organizations are organized around broad themes, appropriate to preschool children, which are drawn from the curriculum areas of all of the program organizations.

Feelings and basic understandings about Christian theology truths begin to lay a foundation for the growing child to develop a valid system of beliefs about God and his relationship to man. On the youth level, many of the units provide assistance in dealing with doubts and reaffirming faith as one's intellectual and social horizons expand. A meaningful emphasis in Christian theology units for adults is finding in Christian theology insights which assist one in dealing with problems and frustrations in everyday life.

An important instrument used in developing life-span training opportunities in the various curriculum areas is the lifelong learning task. By lifelong learning task, we mean a great, general, purposeful lifelong activity engaged in by learners in the educational process. A lifelong learning task helps age-group curriculum planners and church leaders to build on the experiences their members had before they reached their present age level, and to prepare the members for learning experiences they will have later. It also helps to provide at each age level the training experiences needed at that particular time in life.

Lifelong learning tasks for the church training curriculum areas are as follows:

Christian theology—developing a valid system of Christian beliefs about God and his relationship to man.

Christian ethics—growing in Christian character and the ability to express it in every relationship of daily living.

Christian history—discovering and appropriating meaning and values in Christian history.

Church polity and organization—exploring ways in which Baptists work together in achieving Christ's objectives for churches.

Lifelong learning tasks give purpose and unity to the training which the church training program provides persons throughout the life span. At each age level, the curriculum is designed to meet the needs and interests of persons at that point in life. But the total curriculum is so related as to provide a lifetime of meaningful training opportunities. Training for effective Christian discipleship can never be completed. Change may create problems and new problems call for further training or retraining. Churches which speak to the needs of their members, their communities, and their world, discover membership training as a lifetime process.

3. Church Leader Training

What is the most crucial problem your church faces today? This question was raised in a conference of church leaders at Ridgecrest Baptist Assembly. Several serious problems were cited and discussed briefly. The group soon agreed, however, that the most serious problem faced by their churches was the discovery, enlistment, and training of leaders.

There are several reasons for the leadership problem in most churches. As the work of a church expands and develops, there is a corresponding increase in the number of leaders needed. The distressing turnover of leaders creates a large number of vacancies each year. The dramatic increase in the number of unchurched people calls for a large number of leaders to assist in reaching prospects. The increasing complexity of modern life makes it difficult for many people to carry as many church responsibilities as they once carried. These and other factors are creating in churches an unprecedented need for trained lay leaders.

(1) HOW CAN LEADERS BE DISCOVERED?

Every church needs a systematic plan for discovering potential leaders in its membership. Brainstorming, under some circumstances, is a good group technique, but it is an inadequate plan for finding persons to fill leadership vacancies in a Baptist church.

Many churches are finding a talent survey card an excellent plan for discovering potential leaders. When the plan is used, all church members are asked to fill out a card indicating their past leadership experience and their preference for service opportunities. New members fill out a survey card soon after they join the church.

A church directory is another valuable tool for discovering potential leaders. Persons who know the membership well can frequently scan the lists of names of members and discover prospective leaders.

Existing leaders should be encouraged to be on the alert for prospective leaders in their classes or groups. Frequently a Sunday School teacher or a leader of an Adult training group will discover someone in his class or group who has leadership potential. This information should be passed on to the training director.

Some churches appoint talent scouts to search for church members who are holding leadership positions in professional, civic, or social organizations in the community. Often such persons when trained can serve in leadership positions in their church.

Whatever system is used for discovering potential leaders, an adequate filing system for recording and retaining information on prospective leaders is essential.

(2) HOW CAN PROSPECTIVE LEADERS BE RECRUITED?

The quality of leadership is significantly influenced by the way in which leaders are recruited. If told that the job would require little time or effort, they tend to devote little time or effort to it.

The best plan for recruiting leaders is determined partly by the specific persons involved. A few general principles should be kept in mind. One principle is to explain clearly the importance and nature of the work. The expectations the church has of the person filling the position should be made clear. It is important that the person understand the resources available to help him perform his leadership responsibility.

(3) WHO IS RESPONSIBLE FOR LEADERSHIP TRAINING?

For many years, each program organization in Southern Baptist churches was responsible for discovering, enlisting, and training its own lay leaders. A great deal of unhealthy competition and duplication of effort resulted.

Many churches are finding it advantageous to place upon the church training program the responsibility for working with all program organizations in discovering, recruiting, and training leaders.

In the training of lay leaders, church training provides general training for all leaders serving in leadership positions in any of the program organizations. The training of personnel in program administration and specific job skills is the responsibility of each organization. Organizations may request church training to arrange or provide such training. Church training also may take the initiative to offer church program organizations assistance in planning training opportunities and is responsible for providing specialized training to its own leaders.

(4) WHAT KINDS OF TRAINING ARE NEEDED?

Church leader training may be thought of in two phases. They are preservice training and in-service training.

Preservice training is for persons who have never held a church-elected place of service, persons who have not recently held a place of service, and persons who are preparing to accept a different type of leadership assignment.

In-service training is for all persons currently holding church-elected positions. Leaders are assisted in determining their training needs and in securing appropriate training. Additional training, as needed, is provided to enable persons to function effectively in their assignment.

(5) HOW WILL THE TRAINING BE OFFERED?

Most leadership training will be accomplished through group activities. Although not the only type of courses available, the New Church Study Course contains many excellent leadership training courses. Courses in the Christian Leadership series of the New Church Study Course are organized as follows:

General Leadership Training

Introductory courses in church leadership include:

- Courses to help persons understand people of various age levels and people in special groups in a church
- Courses designed to develop general leadership skills

*Specialized Training for Church Programs
and Services*

Bible Teaching Program
Training Program
Church Mission Program—Woman's Missionary Union
Church Mission Program—Brotherhood
Church Music Program
Pastoral Ministries
Program and Administrative Services

An effective leadership training program also provides opportunities for individual study and guidance. The New Church Study Course offers an individual reading program. Internships offer additional training opportunities for individualized training.

The Church Leader Training Section of *Church Training* provides monthly suggestions for persons responsible for leadership training in the church. The purpose of this chapter has been to present an overview of the kinds of training offered in the church training program. Chapter 2 will explain the organization needed to provide this training.

SUMMARY

1. Training is not simply studying about something. Training is a cultivation of understandings, attitudes, and skills necessary to achieve.
2. Training is essential if church members are to fulfil the role of the church in the world.
3. A church must train its members to be resourceful in dealing with unanticipated problems and situations.
4. The church training program offers three types of training for church members: New Church Member Orientation, Church Member Training, and Church Leader Training.
5. All persons received into the fellowship of a church have a special training need.

6. The drastic changes taking place in society make training for Christian living and service a lifelong activity.
7. Church training curriculum areas include Christian theology, Christian ethics, Christian history, and church polity and organization.
8. Every church needs a systematic plan for discovering and training leaders.

Chapter Two

ORGANIZATION
FOR CHURCH TRAINING

ORGANIZATION is a means to an end, not an end in itself. It is a way of grouping people to get a job done. Organization should be a servant, not a master. It is a road, a way, a media—not a goal or an objective. As Louis A. Allen expresses it, "Organization is the process of identifying and grouping the work to be performed, defining and delegating responsibility and authority, and establishing relationships for the purpose of enabling people to work most effectively together in accomplishing objectives." [1]

CRITERIA FOR EFFECTIVE ORGANIZATION

Organization for church training should be effective. There should be no more organization than is needed to accomplish the tasks the church undertakes. The organization should be simple and flexible. That is, it should grow or enlarge as more people are reached or new tasks are assumed. Responsibilities and authority should be clearly stated, understood, and accepted. Each office and unit of organization should exist because there is a task to be done.

1. Louis A. Allen, *Management and Organization* (New York: McGraw-Hill Book Company, 1958), p. 57.

1. *Factors That Influence Organization*

There are certain factors that determine the organization a church will seek to provide for its training program.

(1) AVAILABILITY OF LEADERSHIP. Each church must determine for itself the number of training groups needed and the numbers for which it can provide adequate and capable leadership.

(2) AVAILABILITY OF SPACE. The number and size of rooms influence organization. As more people are reached for training, the church will need to provide adequate space. Preschoolers and Children usually should meet in the same rooms on Sunday evening as on Sunday morning.

(3) TOTAL POTENTIAL ENROLMENT IN AN AGE SPAN. The potential enrolment includes those enrolled and those likely to be enrolled. A church composed primarily of young adults would have need for a higher ratio of Preschool and Children's departments than a church made up primarily of older adults.

The number of persons in each age group is a factor for consideration in organization. The number of persons in each group will determine which ages will be grouped together in a department. It is not necessary to have the same age span in each department. Nor is it necessary to maintain the same grouping of ages year after year.

GROUPING AND GRADING PLANS

In October 1970 all Southern Baptist church programs, Sunday School, Training Union, Church Music, Woman's Missionary Union, and Brotherhood, introduced a new grouping and grading plan. This plan is so constructed as to allow churches to adapt their organizational plans according to their particular needs. It also provides for grading Children and Youth in close relation to public school systems. The chart on page 18 shows four patterns of grouping. A church should choose the pattern or patterns which best meets their needs.

Pattern 1 is designed for the small church where it may be necessary or desirable to place all persons within a division in one group. *Pattern 4* is designed for the larger church which may have one

RECOMMENDED GROUPING—GRADING SYSTEM

DIVISION TITLES	Divisional Grouping Patterns			
	I.	II.**	III.**	IV.**
PRESCHOOL DIVISION	Birth–1	B–1	B–1	B–1
	1*	1	1	1
	2	2	2	2
	3*	3	3	3
	4	4	4	4
	5*	5	5	5
CHILDREN'S DIVISION	6 (Grade 1)	6	6	6
	7 (Grade 2)*	7	7	7
	8 (Grade 3)	8	8	8
	9 (Grade 4)*	9	9	9
	10 (Grade 5)	10	10	10
	11 (Grade 6)*	11	11	11
YOUTH DIVISION	12 (Grade 7)	12	12	12
	13 (Grade 8)*	13	13	13
	14 (Grade 9)	14	14	14
	15 (Grade 10)*	15	15	15
	16 (Grade 11)	16	16	16
	17 (Grade 12)*	17	17	17
ADULT DIVISION		18 (or high school graduation)	18 (or high school graduation)	18 (or high school graduation) 1
		Young Adult	Young Adult 1 2	Young Adult 2 / 3
		29	29	29 4
	18 (high school graduation) and up	30	30	30 1
		Adult	Adult 1 2	Adult 2 / 3
		59 (or retirement)	59 (or retirement)	59 (or retirement) 4
		60 (or retirement)	60 (or retirement)	60 (or retirement) 1
		Senior Adult	Senior Adult 1 2	Senior Adult 2 / 3
				4

*These ages will serve as the centers for planning and offering curriculum materials to the churches for use with the patterns they select.

**Additional departments should be added on the basis of possibilities in terms of classifications: college students, single or married persons, age.

or more departments for each year or school grade. A church might choose to follow one pattern for one division and another pattern for another division. An example of this might be a suburban church with many children and few adults. It might follow *Pattern 3* for the Children's Division and *Pattern 2* for the Adult.

PATTERNS OF ORGANIZATION

Each church is encouraged to analyze its training needs and determine the amount and kind of organization required. The church should then move courageously and in faith to organize to meet its needs. Several patterns of organization are suggested to help a church in establishing its training organization. Each general pattern can be adapted to meet more specific needs.

In a comprehensive training program, organization is needed for three types of training: New Church Member Orientation, Church Member Training, and Church Leader Training. For the churches which now have only member training (with the director of church training responsible for the training), at least one organizational unit is needed for each of the other two types. This can be as simple as designating one additional person to be responsible for each of the other types. Pattern 1 describes this organization.

Pattern 1 provides for at least one training unit in each of the three types of training. This pattern makes easy the expansion of the number of units of each type.

By scheduling the training at different times, fewer persons can carry on the program. For example, new member orientation may be conducted on Sunday morning, Sunday evening, or at convenient weekday hours. Leader training may be conducted on Sunday or during the week.

The organization suggested in pattern 1 is recommended:

1. When there is at least one training group or class in each of the three types of training; or
2. When the director of church training can administer the training done in all three types of training; or
3. When members, prospects, leaders, leadership training, and space are limited; or

4. When each of the four age divisions has at least one member training department or group.

PATTERN 1

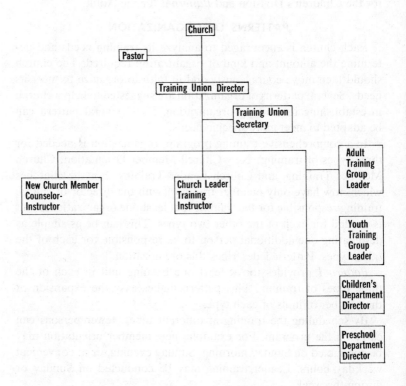

Pattern 2 is suggested for churches which need more organization than is indicated in pattern 1. Pattern 2 calls for more than one unit of organization but does not require general directors for these additional types of training. This pattern also allows for Adult and Youth departments and multiple units in those departments. The director and secretary of church training would have the same responsibilities as in pattern 1.

Pattern 2 is recommended:

1. When there is at least one department, training group, or class in each of the three types of training; or
2. When there is need and leadership available to provide graded new church member orientation for children; or
3. When more than one level of leader training needs to be provided; or
4. When more than one training group is needed in each Adult and Youth member training department.

PATTERN 2

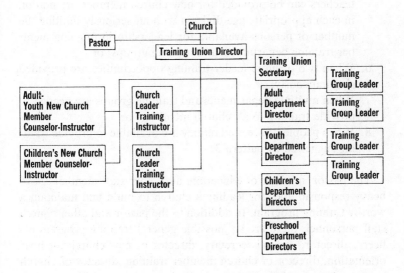

Pattern 3 is recommended for churches which offer a more comprehensive training program than those of patterns 1 and 2. Pattern 3 offers many variations and identifies relationships and functions in a comprehensive church training program.

The organization in pattern 3 is recommended:

1. When the church has a person on its professional staff to give direction to the church's total education program; or
2. When it appears advisable to have a person to plan and coordinate all enlistment activities for the total training program; or
3. When the director of church training feels the need for assistance in administering the total program; or
4. When there is need and leadership available to provide new church member orientation for each age division—Adult, Youth, and Children; or
5. When the leadership potential is such that a counselor and teachers can be provided for new church member orientation in each appropriate age division without seriously limiting the number of persons available for leadership in ongoing member training departments and training groups; or
6. When two or more leader training opportunities are provided simultaneously; or
7. When multiple departments and training groups are needed to provide training to all church members; or
8. When people, space, and money are available to provide training suggested by pattern 3.

The pastor, minister of education, and other staff members have heavy responsibilities for leading a church to build and maintain a worthy training program. In addition to the pastor and other church staff personnel, there are six possible general training program officers: director, general secretary, director of new church member orientation, director of church member training, director of church leader training, and director of enlistment.

The duties of a particular officer are the same in all three organizational patterns. If a person serves in two of these positions, he is responsible for the duties of both positions.

The duties of each general officer are described in detail in chapter 3.

PATTERN 3

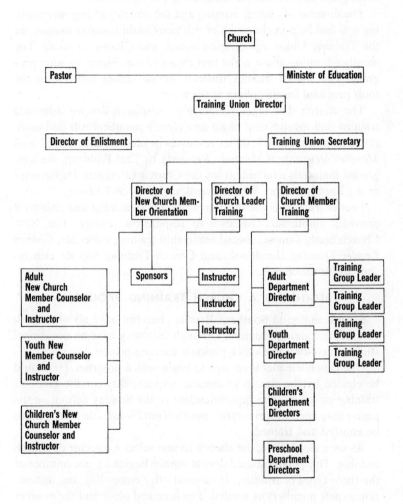

The three-pronged approach to training—new member, member, and leader—had its beginning in the 1950's, grew in the 1960's, and holds great possibilities for the churches of the 1970's.

The director of church training and the director of member training will find help in chapter 8 of this book. Additional resources are the Training Union age-division books, and *Church Training*. The member training phase is the first thrust of the church training program. The church training director should secure and master the tools provided for this phase of the work.

The church that takes seriously its responsibility for adequate training and involvement of all new church members will find additional help in chapter 7. Other resources needed are the *New Church Member Orientation Manual* (*Revised*) by Earl Waldrup, the age-graded materials available from the Church Literature Department of the Baptist Sunday School Board, and *Church Training*.

Leader training is the third area of church training and chapter 9 provides additional assistance to responsible leaders. The New Church Study Course, special leadership training materials, *Church Leader Training Handbook,* and *Church Training* provide rich resources for the church.

BEGINNING A CHURCH TRAINING PROGRAM

Several thousand Southern Baptist churches have no organized, continuing training program, although they may have an occasional study course or some other periodic training project.

One capable leader is enough to begin such a program. He should be elected by the church to assume responsibility for the church's training program. The superintendent of the Sunday School or the pastor may need to serve in this position until some other person can be enlisted and trained.

As soon as possible, the church should select a director of church training. This person should devote time to beginning one or more of the three types of training. He should offer counseling and instruction to new members as needed. The time and place and the number of training sessions would be determined by the needs of the persons involved.

The director of church training should offer some short-term training for church members, selecting study materials from the periodicals and resource units. The needs and interests of the study group would determine the selection of materials. Since there is always a need for more and better trained leaders, the director of church training could start with leader training, using some of the special leader training materials or training materials from the New Church Study Course.

Organization chart 1 shows the organization needed for a church beginning a training program.

ORGANIZATION CHART 1

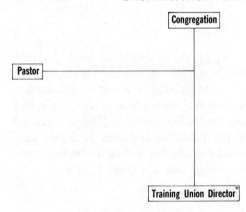

In this particular organization the director of church training would assume the appropriate duties described in the preceding paragraphs. The pastor would be involved directly with the church training director in planning and conducting training opportunities.

Another approach to the beginning of a training program in a church is to provide each type of training within an age-group department. For example, a small church which has only one adult department could have a member training group, a new church member class, and a leader training class within the department. Organization chart 2 presents this arrangement.

---

* Could be the director of the Bible teaching program.

ORGANIZATION CHART 2

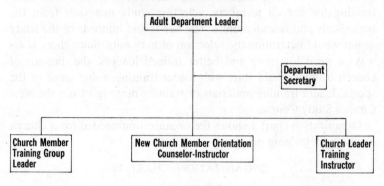

In the Children's Division, provision should be made for new member orientation of children who join the church. The department director or leader would provide training as a part of the department's work. This could be done individually or in groups, depending on the number involved and leadership available. The younger the child, the greater the need for individual attention. A similar plan might be used in the Youth Division. For the entire training program, the basic organization might look like chart 3, page 27.

SUMMARY

1. Organization is a means to an end, not an end in itself.
2. Each office and unit of organization should exist because there is a task to be done.
3. Each church should analyze its training needs and determine the amount and kind of organization required.
4. One interested and capable person is enough to begin a training program in a church.
5. New Member Training and Leader Training can be offered within ongoing Church Member Training departments.

ORGANIZATION CHART 3

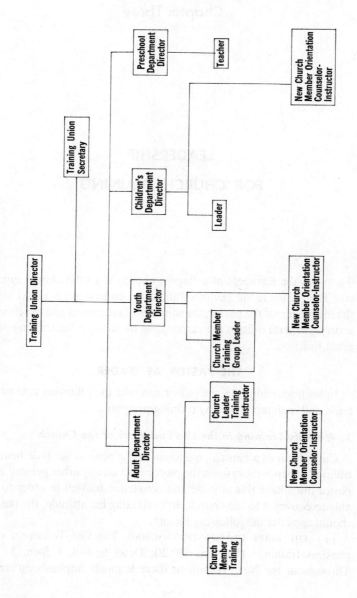

Training Union Director

Training Union Secretary

Adult Department Director

Youth Department Director

Children's Department Director

Preschool Department Director

Teacher

Leader

Church Leader Training Instructor

Church Member Training Group Leader

New Church Member Orientation Counselor-Instructor

New Church Member Orientation Counselor-Instructor

New Church Member Orientation Counselor-Instructor

Church Member Training

Chapter Three

LEADERSHIP

FOR CHURCH TRAINING

TRAINING the members of a Baptist church is a total church ministry. The pastor is the leader of all of the church ministries. Under
the leadership of the pastor, the minister of education and the church
training general officers are responsible for making the training program function.

THE PASTOR AS LEADER

In his leadership role, the pastor can take the following actions to
build and maintain a worthy training program.

1. Magnify Training in the Life and Work of the Church

Cultivation of a church conviction and a positive attitude toward
training depends more upon the pastor than on any other person. The
pastor must have this attitude and conviction himself in order to be
able to convey it to the church. In evaluating his attitude, the pastor
should consider the following factors:

(1) THE BIBLE COMMANDS TRAINING. The Old Testament emphasizes training: (See Ex. 18:20; Deut. 6:4–9; 1 Sam. 3:1.)
Throughout the New Testament there is much emphasis on train-

28

ing. (See Matt. 28:19–20; Luke 10:1–12; 11:1; Acts 16:1–5; Eph. 4:11–16; 1 Tim. 4:13–14; 2 Tim. 2:15.) Baptists are Bible people. Whatever the Bible commands is not optional. It is imperative.

(2) BAPTIST PRINCIPLES DEMAND TRAINING. The nature of our Baptist principles demands training. The great Baptist principle of the competency of the individual soul, under God, to deal directly with God in all matters of religion emphasizes the infinite worth of every soul and the necessity for full spiritual development for every person. The democracy of a Baptist church requires individual participation, and individual participation requires individual development. People must be trained to participate. Our doctrine of the open Bible requires that every person shall become proficient in Bible knowledge and skilful in using God's Word.

(3) THE CHRISTIAN'S NEED FOR SPIRITUAL GROWTH REQUIRES TRAINING. People come into the kingdom of God by way of the spiritual birth. When they enter, they are spiritual babes. To develop maturity in the Christian life, each one must grow. It is the business of each church to provide the means of growth for each one of its members. This it tries to do through the training program.

(4) THE CHURCH'S NEED FOR WORKERS MAKES TRAINING IMPERATIVE. God has a work for every church member. Not all are called to be teachers or leaders. God challenges each one to serve. Church training seeks to make every member available for service. Under the leadership of the Holy Spirit, those who should lead should be called into that service.

2. Place Church Training Activities in the Church Calendar

The pastor is chairman of the church council, made up of the heads of all church organizations. This group should plan a church calendar for the total church program. The pastor should see that church training events and activities are scheduled properly.

3. Lead the Church to Build Its Training Program

Intelligent leadership requires that the pastor keep abreast of training progress. The church should purchase and place in the pastor's library copies of ADMINISTERING CHURCH TRAINING, age-division leadership books, and *The Association and Church Training*. Training Union periodicals should also be provided for the pastor each quarter.

The church itself is responsible for building its training program. This means that the pastor must lead in this great project. There are certain areas in which his leadership and influence must be brought to bear.

(1) PROVIDING CAPABLE LEADERSHIP. If the church can have a minister of education, the pastor should lead in seeing that one is added to the church staff. The church staff should lead the church nominating committee to see that the church training program has one of the best leaders of the church to serve as director. In the selection of all leaders and workers the pastor's counsel is indispensable. The church nominating committee and the director of church training should keep in close touch with the pastor in this matter.

(2) EXPANDING AND STRENGTHENING THE ORGANIZATION. The pastor should guide in enlarging the church training program. He should have a clear conception of the kind of organization needed and then guide the church in building it. It is the pastor's privilege to inspire his leadership to build a worthy training program.

(3) ENLIST THE CHURCH MEMBERS. Church training is a family affair. There is a place in the church training program for all members of the church and their families. The pastor's influence is powerful enough to convince all the deacons and all the members of the church that they should be in the church training program. His word at this point makes easier the task of the church training leadership in enlisting the people to participate.

(4) BUILDING TO MEET TRAINING NEEDS. Every church should build to take care of its total educational program. This means that it will build for a church training program as well as for a Bible teaching program.

The state convention Church Training department and the Church Training Department of the Baptist Sunday School Board will help pastors know completely the needs for the church training program in church building.

(5) HELPING CHURCH TRAINING LEADERS WITH THEIR PROBLEMS. The pastor should attend the church training council meeting in order to know all of the needs and the problems of his church training leadership. He should make himself available at specific times to counsel with these leaders and assist them in meeting needs and solving problems.

4. Use Training Union in Building the Total Church Program

A dynamic Training Union vitalizes the whole church program. The church training program is an available force for the pastor to use in building the total church program. Here are a few of the ways in which it can serve:

(1) BUILDING THE SUNDAY EVENING SERVICE AND THE CHURCH PRAYER MEETING. Training Union is the pastor's helper in the total Sunday evening program. Any church which has a functioning training program can have a great Sunday evening service. The same is true of the midweek prayer meeting. The pastor should lead his church training leadership to help him build the prayer meeting.

(2) TRAINING PERSONAL SOUL-WINNERS. One of the finest ways to get ready for a revival in a Baptist church is to conduct graded training sessions for all church members, using good training materials. This training should be conducted three or four weeks before the revival. All of the church members should be urged to participate. Names of lost people should be assigned to the various age groups for visitation during these training sessions. It should be a practical laboratory in soul-winning.

(3) CONSERVING THE RESULTS OF EVANGELISM. The church training program provides orientation for new church members.

(4) RAISING THE CHURCH BUDGET. The church training program is an available stewardship force in every Baptist church. Each year, when the church seeks to pledge its budget, full publicity should be given the church training program.

(5) DEVELOPING WORKERS FOR ALL THE CHURCH MINISTRIES.

The church training program should be a perennial source of supply for workers for all of the church ministries. Deacons, Sunday School teachers, mission program leaders, and personal workers are developed in Training Union. Through the method of individual participation in all Training Union work, workers are made available for other places of service.

LAYMEN AS LEADERS

Every Christian has an opportunity to become a more useful member of his world. The New Testament teaches that all Christians are to have a definite part in fulfilling the mission of their church. The call to discipleship is a call to serve, to develop and use one's gifts. The call to serve charges those persons with exceptional gifts, insights, and/or training to use these assets to assist their church toward its spiritual goals.

These goals may be stated in terms of developing understandings, skills, and attitudes essential to effective discipleship. The Training Union has the primary responsibility of developing new leaders and better prepared members. Leaders for this program should possess certain personal qualifications.

QUALIFICATIONS OF LEADERS

The specific job assignment will determine the leadership skills a person will need. However, all leaders should possess certain basic characteristics. Some jobs will demand more than others and these will be singled out for particular emphasis.

1. A Church Training Leader Should Be:

(1) A MATURING CHRISTIAN. Experiencing the new birth is basic to all service, but a leader should give evidence of an increasing awareness of the presence and power of God in his life and of a continuing maturing relationship with God.

(2) A LOYAL AND INFORMED CHURCH MEMBER. A leader should have a working knowledge of the total program of his church, believe in the program, and give it his wholehearted support.

(3) A DEPENDABLE WORKER. In his leadership role, he should be fully aware that his failure *to do* or *to be* can handicap the work of Christ and damage the lives of other Christians. He should seek to prepare himself and to efficiently carry out every assignment.

(4) A WILLING LEARNER. Every leader should be willing to learn and to recognize his own need to continually improve himself.

(5) AN ENTHUSIASTIC LEADER. Enthusiasm is the source from which growth and activity spring. Enthusiasm is that infectious element which makes the difference between dutiful performance and energetic achievement.

(6) ONE WHO LOVES PEOPLE. The desire to see people grow as useful, happy Christians can help a leader overcome fears, frustrations, and disappointments. This desire also gives him purpose in what he does.

(7) A STUDENT OF THE BIBLE. Possessing a working knowledge of the Word and understanding its basic teachings is essential to effective work.

(8) DEDICATED TO SACRIFICIAL SERVICE. A leader should be willing to "pay a price" in service. He should know the goals toward which he is working and possess the willingness to pay the price for achievement.

2. A Church Training Leader Should Be Able to:

(1) COMMUNICATE. His responsibilities include presiding, speaking, and leading devotional activities.

(2) ADMINISTER. Planning, organizing, and evaluating are responsibilities of a leader.

(3) INSTRUCT. He should be familiar with the learning process, the use of instructional techniques, the preparation of learning aids, and the methods for involving people in learning experiences.

(4) DEMONSTRATE. He should be aware that his personal witnessing, visiting, enlisting, and ministering will have tremendous bearing on his effectiveness with others.

(5) COUNSEL. The leader needs skill in listening, analyzing, sensing needs, and understanding and accepting people.

DUTIES OF CHURCH TRAINING LEADERS

The job descriptions which follow suggest the degree to which a leader may need to possess or develop the skills mentioned in the preceding section. The lack of skills should not be an acceptable reason for rejecting a prospective worker or for his refusal to consider serving.

Acceptance of a job should be dependent upon the training and guidance necessary for performing the assigned responsibilities. The training should begin at the point of the most obvious deficiencies.

Some of the distinctive needs of general officers are listed with their job descriptions.

1. *Director*

(1) PERSONAL QUALIFICATIONS

Christian maturity
Dedication to service
Broad knowledge of church's life and work
Understanding of the teaching-learning process
Knowledge and appreciation of training program, with special skills in communication, interpersonal and intergroup relations, group dynamics, Christian education, and administration

The director of the church training program is responsible to the congregation for planning, directing, and coordinating the church's training program. In his reporting relationships, he also works with the pastor and minister of education.

(2) DUTIES

a. Serve on the church council to represent church training needs in the planning of the church program
b. Serve as chairman of the church training council and lead the council in planning, recommending, conducting, and evaluating the training program
c. Recommend improvements in policies, procedures, and activities for the church training program

d. Lead the church council and the church in planning, promoting, and evaluating a comprehensive training program

e. Recommend and train directors for each type of training and work with them in recommending and training other training program leaders

f. Recommend the budget for the church training program

g. Work with the directors of each type of training in planning, conducting, and evaluating the training program in their areas

h. Assign responsibility within the training program for family ministry, vocational guidance, and other church emphases and projects, as requested by the church

i. Provide organization, leadership, and other resources for short-term training projects related to church goals, special emphases, or individual needs or interest

If the director also serves as director of one or more of the types of training, the duties recommended for that director become a part of his specific duties.

2. Secretary

The secretary is responsible to the director for preparing the records and reports needed in the overall operation of a church training program.

(1) DUTIES

a. Serve on the council and help plan, recommend, conduct, and evaluate the church training program

b. Compile general records and reports needed by the director, council, other leadership groups, and the church in planning, conducting, and evaluating the training program

c. Compile requests for literature and supplies needed in the different units of the training organization and relay the needs to the proper officer for ordering

d. Distribute all literature and supplies to the appropriate training units

e. Advise other training unit secretaries in the preparation and maintenance of proper records

f. Maintain individual training records and provide training information to officers and members as requested

g. Request, receive, and post all church study course awards

h. Supervise the classification and enrolment of new members and remove names from the rolls according to the church's enrolment policies

i. Make appropriate reports to the church training council and other planning groups

3. *Director of New Member Orientation*

The personal qualifications and needs of this officer are similar to those listed for the director of the entire church training program.

The director of new member orientation is responsible to the director of church training for planning, directing, and evaluating the new member orientation program for the church.

He should be familiar with the book *New Church Member Orientation Manual* (*Revised*), the age-graded materials, and the New Church Member Orientation Section of *Church Training*.

(1) DUTIES

a. Lead the church in planning, conducting, coordinating and promoting orientation for new church members

b. Work with the new church member sponsors, counselors, instructors, and secretaries in planning and conducting their work

c. Secure substitutes when regular new church member orientation workers are absent

d. Seek meaningful involvement of new members in the life of the church and its witness to the world

e. Guide other church leaders, church members, and members of their families in the life and work of the church

f. Serve on the church training council and help plan, recommend, and evaluate the entire church training program (responsibilities of new church member counselor-instructor in patterns 1 and 2)

g. Recommend to the director of church training the budget for literature, supplies, and other expenses *h*. Work with the director of member training to insure further training and involvement of new members after completion of new member orientation

i. Work with the director of church leader training to equip, train, and counsel other new member orientation workers

j. Evaluate new church member orientation and recommend improvements

k. Assign appropriate responsibility within the new church member orientation organization for family ministry, vocational guidance, and other church emphases and special projects, as requested by the director of Training Union

4. Director of Church Member Training

The director of church member training is responsible to the director of Training Union for planning, conducting, and evaluating member training for the church.

(1) DUTIES

a. Serve on the Training Union council and help plan, recommend, conduct, and evaluate the church training program

b. Lead the church in planning, conducting, and evaluating church member training—including continuing age-graded training and short-term training to meet special needs

c. Serve as coordinator of special training projects for church members, such as Operation Home Study, Backyard Studies, etc.

d. Work with leaders of organizational units in planning, conducting, and evaluating their training activities

e. Work with director of enlistment in seeking the enlistment of church members in church member training

f. Work with the secretary to maintain accurate records of credits and certificates earned in the New Church Study Course

g. Recommend prospective member training leaders and work with the director of leader training in providing specialized training to equip them for effective service

h. Assign responsibility for family ministry, vocational guidance, and other church emphases or projects, as requested by the director of church training

i. Recommend to the director of church training the budget for literature, supplies, and other member training expenses

j. Evaluate church member training and recommend improvements in policies, procedures, and activities

5. *Director of Church Leader Training*

The director of church leader training is responsible to the director of church training for planning, conducting, and evaluating church leader training.

(1) DUTIES

a. Serve on the church training council and help plan, recommend, conduct, and evaluate the church training program

b. Lead the church to discover its leader training needs in cooperation with the director of church training and the church council

c. Work with training officers in other church programs to determine training needs and best schedules for training

d. Lead in planning, conducting, and evaluating leader training (responsibilities of church leader training instructor in patterns 1 and 2)

e. Serve as coordinator of special leader training projects

f. Publicize all leader training projects and list individuals to participate

g. Lead in discovering, recruiting, and training potential leaders

h. Plan appropriate recognition for persons participating in church leader training

i. Recommend leaders for leader training organization and provide training needed by them

j. Recommend to the director of church training the budget for literature, supplies, and other church leader training expenses (responsibilities of church leader instructor in patterns 1 and 2)

k. Evaluate church leader training and recommend improvements in policies, procedures, and activities (responsibilities of church leader instructor in patterns 1 and 2)

l. Provide organization and leadership for short-term leader training projects related to church goals, emphases, and special projects, as requested by the director of church training

6. Director of Enlistment

The director of enlistment is responsible to the director of church training for planning, conducting, and evaluating the enlistment of church members in the church training program. In organizations not having this position, the director of church training is responsible for carrying out these duties or assigning them to others.

(1) DUTIES

a. Serve on the church training council and help plan, recommend, conduct, and evaluate the church training program

b. Keep an up-to-date list of training prospects in the church, including prospect lists for each training unit

c. Assign prospects to appropriate units of the church training organization for enlistment

d. Plan, conduct, and evaluate a regular visitation program to reach prospects and absentees

e. Work with the directors of each type of training and the secretary to receive, classify, and assign new members to appropriate units of organization

f. Plan the reception and assignment of visitors to appropriate units of the training organization

g. Seek the meaningful involvement of all church members in the life and witness of the church

ENLISTING LEADERS

We have considered the question of the types of leaders needed and the special skills they should possess. The next logical question is where to find these leaders.

1. LEADERS MAY BE FOUND IN THE MEMBER TRAINING PROGRAM. Adults and older youth are potential leaders. Church members should know that their efforts are appreciated and that their service is needed. The member training program should encourage the desire for increased responsibility. Morale is usually improved if someone from within the organization can be chosen to lead.

2. LEADERS CAN BE DISCOVERED THROUGH THE LEADER TRAINING PROGRAM. An effective leader training program will produce leaders capable of more specialized training. This training can be administered as "on-the-job" training. Leaders who have completed introductory general leader training courses should be considered as "interns" or associates for a period of time in order to gain experience.

3. LEADERS CAN BE FOUND OUTSIDE THE TRAINING PROGRAM. Surveys of the membership can help discover additional sources of leaders. Special effort should be made to discover potential leaders among adults not presently involved in training. Results of the surveys should be preserved for future enlistment efforts.

4. LEADERS MIGHT BE FOUND IN NEW CHURCH MEMBER ORIENTATION. New transfer members may have a great deal of leadership potential. Even a new convert may have the experience and maturity needed in some situations.

Leaders serving in other programs should be considered for the church training program. The rotation of workers among programs helps to achieve balance of interest and leads additional persons into training. Enlisting leaders is an individual task, but it must ultimately have the approval of the church. Every church needs an enlistment process which will prevent a competitive atmosphere from developing between organizations. The church nominating committee should work out the specific procedures. It may be sufficient to suggest that the Training Union director, department directors, church staff members, and the nominating committee agree on a plan and procedure.

ORIENTING LEADERS

A new leader needs special instruction, encouragement, and guidance if he is to function satisfactorily. He must become acquainted with his fellow workers and with the members of his group. He must know his various responsibilities.

This induction into leadership need not be a formal process. However, all workers are worthy of recognition and appreciation. An effort should be made to either present new leaders in a planning meeting or to plan a fellowship for all leaders. An annual or semi-annual leadership supper is one way of helping leaders to become better acquainted.

Every church should have a plan for recognizing the beginning of service. The election of new leaders can be an announcement in the church newspaper. It may be an occasion of fellowship and challenge, such as an installation service as a part of the regular church worship service.

Leader orientation for service is essential to good work. Every new leader needs:

- An overview of the entire church training program

- An understanding of his relationship to the total church training program

- An understanding of the schedule of activities he is expected to follow, channels of communication, and relevant church policies and procedures

A new worker should study the texts relating to his job. He should also receive specific help in his job responsibilities. There are textbooks available which deal with understanding age levels and with the best learning methods to use with groups. However, more is required if the worker is to understand his specific duties.

Curriculum and supplemental materials which the new leaders will use need to be identified and their use explained. Many leaders are not aware of the resources available.

TRAINING AND DEVELOPING

Functioning in a job is training in itself, yet the effectiveness with which leaders perform their duties will depend to a great extent on the opportunities for training and development offered them. The development of leaders is the administrative responsibility of the training program. The training of each worker is the responsibility of the particular organization leader. This does not mean that the responsible leader himself must conduct the training. It means that he must see that needed training is made available. The resources of the church leader training program as outlined in chapter 9 are available to help the responsible leader with this responsibility.

Development begins with evaluation or analysis of the leader's abilities and needs. Basic information thus gained provides a yardstick by which to measure the impact of the training program. It provides an incentive for personal development and a measure of the individual's success. The qualities, understandings, and skills needed by leaders of the church training program have been listed earlier. These lists will serve as valuable guides in helping a leader discover his needs for further training.

An evaluation may reveal that training of one of the following types is needed:

1. REMEDIAL TRAINING—to meet the leader's need for additional training in a particular area or to provide retraining because of changes in work assignment, methods, or procedures.
2. SKILL TRAINING—to provide for skill development beyond that which is considered essential to meeting minimum job requirements.

If it is discovered that a leader is lacking in background in any of the subject areas listed under leader training in chapter 9, he may be encouraged to take one or more courses in that particular area. Ideally, a person should have completed general training as pre-service training. However, these courses can be taken as in-service training through either group or individual training approaches.

In addition to making training available, a responsible leader can do much through personal counseling and guidance to develop those persons who serve with him. He can also challenge and teach by being a good example of what a dedicated, effective, and growing leader should be.

SUMMARY

1. The New Testament teaches that all church members are to be a part of fulfilling the mission of his church.
2. The specific job assignment will determine the leadership skills a person needs.
3. The Training Union director is responsible for planning, directing, and coordinating the total church training program.
4. The general officers of the training program, and in many churches also department directors, comprise the council.
5. The director of enlistment is responsible for leading the total enlistment program of church training.
6. New leaders need instruction, encouragement, and guidance if they are to function satisfactorily.
7. The development of leaders for the church training program is the responsibility of the Training Union director.
8. Leaders already in service may need additional training while they serve.

Chapter Four

CHURCH TRAINING
RESOURCES

PHYSICAL RESOURCES needed for a training program include space, equipment, and supplies. Each church program organization must be considered as it shares in the total program of the church. Space, equipment, and supplies may be used by two or more church program organizations. Each program organization should determine the physical resources needed for its own distinctive program of work.

CURRICULUM MATERIALS AND SUPPLIES

Curriculum materials, promotional materials, and record forms are expendable materials—called supplies—used in the administration or activity of the church training program. We shall consider each of them, their importance, and their place in the total church training program.

The Holy Spirit is the most valuable single resource in Christian education. It is he who motivates, guides, and makes permanent all meaningful learning. Without his help, no real learning can take place.

Even with the help of the Holy Spirit, there is the need of a long-range curriculum plan to give structure to the training process. For training groups to meet week after week without having a basic curriculum plan would result in wasted efforts, lack of achievement, and frustration. The basic design or curriculum plan for the church training program is found in a wide variety of attractive and educationally sound curriculum materials.

Early in the 1960's, denominational personnel began work on the curriculum plans for the training materials to be introduced in the churches in October 1970. Many trained curriculum specialists spent hundreds of hours developing curriculum plans. The aim of these plans was to give adequate structure for training in the churches while providing enough flexibility to meet the needs of a specific church. Also included in the aim was the provision for individual learners to receive appropriate attention. The elements which go into these curriculum plans are too numerous and complex to be described in detail in this context. Examples of these elements, however, are the lifelong learning tasks and continuing learning activities described in chapter 1.

1. The Purpose of Curriculum Materials

Before considering the curriculum materials available for use in the church training program, one needs first to understand the specific function of curriculum materials.

Some people are not aware of the distinction between curriculum materials and curriculum itself. *Curriculum* is something which happens in real-life learning situations. A group, for example, studied a unit entitled "Overcoming Barriers in Race Relations." The curriculum was not the unit itself, but the knowledge, attitude, appreciation, and skill acquired as a result of the study. Specifically, *curriculum* is the sum of all learning experiences resulting from a curriculum plan used under church guidance and directed toward attaining a church's objectives.

Curriculum materials are tools, or resources, for leaders and learners to use in stimulating and guiding learning activities and experiences. Like other tools, they should be used with good judgment and in keeping with the purpose of the tools themselves. Curriculum materials should never be a substitute for individual initiative or hard work on the part of leaders and learners. A curriculum periodical is designed to open up avenues for exploration and to stimulate and guide study. It is not intended to be a crutch to compensate for inadequate planning.

2. The Range of Curriculum Materials

Several kinds of curriculum materials are provided for use in stimulating and guiding training experiences in the church training program. Church leaders who direct the program of training need to be familiar with all of these materials if they are to help their associates select and use the materials most appropriate for their respective departments and groups.

CURRICULUM PERIODICALS—MEMBER TRAINING

Division	Title	Organizational Units Using Periodical
Preschool (Birth–5)	Guide A for Preschool Teachers	Younger departments
	Guide B for Preschool Teachers	Middle departments
	Guide C for Preschool Teachers	Older departments
Children (6–11) (Grades 1–6)	Exploring A	Younger departments
	Exploring A for Leaders	Younger departments
	Exploring B	Middle departments
	Exploring B for Leaders	Middle departments
	Exploring C	Older departments
	Exploring C for Leaders	Older departments
Youth (12–17) (Grades 7–12)	Alive	Younger groups
	Alive for Leaders	Younger groups
	Becoming	Middle groups
	Becoming for Leaders	Middle groups
	Care	Older groups
	Care for Leaders	Older groups

Adult	*Source*	Any adult group
(18–up)	*Source for Leaders*	Any adult group
(Above high	*Source Digest*	Any adult group
school)		(Contents in easy-to-read digest form)
	Skill	Any adult group
	Skill for Leaders	Any adult group
	Now	Any adult group
	Now for Leaders	Any adult group
	La Fe Bautista	Spanish-speaking adults

. . . .

General	*Church Training*	General officers

The curriculum materials for use in member training are attractive periodicals for leaders and members of the various divisions of the church training program. Titles of the periodicals and the age groups for which they are intended are shown on the chart. The leadership periodicals carry resources for leaders of divisions, departments, and groups.

Resource units and other types of elective studies for use in member training are published from time to time to meet special needs. A listing of these special study materials appears on the church literature order form.

Attractive curriculum supplements and picture sets are designed to enrich study units in the membership materials. They also appear on the church literature order form and may be ordered from the Church Literature Department of the Baptist Sunday School Board. Additional resources for church training activities may be ordered from this same source. For example, *The Church Recreation Magazine* could help enrich fellowship. Material produced by The Program of Family Ministry and The Program of Vocational Guidance would help meet special needs.

The New Church Study Course provides additional training resources for church members and church leaders. One phase in the study course, designed for use in member training, is the Christian Development Courses. This series of courses is designed to offer church members more comprehensive, more advanced, and/or more varied learning experiences than is provided in curriculum periodicals.

The second phase of the New Church Study Course is designed for training leaders. The Christian Leadership Courses can be used for training groups and individuals.

The New Church Study Course is an inter-program training plan designed for use in all programs and services.

Additional resources for leader training are available in *Church Training; Skill for Leaders;* and other special training materials.

A comprehensive list of member and leader materials also are available for use in the orientation of new members. Titles, each with a member's book and a leader's book, are *Promises to Keep* (for children's groups), *Belonging* (for youth groups), and *In Covenant* (for adult groups).

3. The Effective Use of Curriculum Resources

Many people spend hundreds of hours preparing the curriculum materials available for use in the church training program. Their efforts bring the best results when the materials are used effectively in the churches.

Pastors, church training directors, and other general officers can do several things to improve the use of curriculum materials in their churches.

One of the most important things they can do is to assist department and group leaders in securing the appropriate curriculum materials for use in their organizational units. A survey of reader reactions to Training Union materials in 1968, revealed that scores of workers were not even aware of all of the curriculum materials available for use in their departments and unions. It is the responsibility of the general officers to become familiar with all church training curriculum materials and to see that they are being used properly in their church.

General officers, especially pastors and church training directors, can also help by calling attention to special study opportunities. When outlines for a full year are published and again when new materials are received each quarter, general officers should preview the training opportunities and identify ones of special merit. These special training units should be called to the attention of age-group workers. The workers should be encouraged to make plans to use these special training units.

General officers should encourage adequate planning. Careful advance planning is essential to successful training. Not only should a regular plan for training be developed, but general officers should encourage and assist age-group workers in taking advantage of planning opportunities.

Age-group workers frequently need help in securing supplementary materials and supplies to enrich training. General officers can provide this help by seeing that funds are available in the budget for purchasing needed items, by helping to develop the church library as a resource center, and by encouraging age-group workers to procure the special materials they need.

Pastors and church training directors especially have an opportunity to work with age-group leaders in publicizing special training opportunities. Frequently, an announcement from the pulpit concerning a special study unit will do more to attract attention to the study then anything the age-group workers can do.

Finally, general officers have an opportunity and responsibility for encouraging age-group workers to use curriculum resources effectively. Encouraging words from the pastor and church training director can stimulate many age-group workers to make far better use of the curriculum resources they have at their disposal.

In the church which does not have a church library, training program leaders should lead in starting one. Space should be provided and designated for the storing of training materials which may be used at other times in appropriate training opportunities. Materials stored in such space (church library or other space) should be classified and clearly labeled. The label should identify the contents, giving the date it was used, and the name of the organization using it.

(1) RECORD FORMS. The general director of the training program in consultation with other leaders of the training program, should determine the types of record forms to be used. Requests for

an ample supply of these forms should be made according to the church plan. Record forms to meet the needs of churches of various sizes are available from your Baptist Book Store.

(2) PROMOTIONAL MATERIALS. A supply of promotional materials related to the training program should be included in the supplies on hand. Some promotional materials interpret new or modified phases of the church's training program; others contain suggestions which can help to make existing phases of the program more effective.

Promotional materials also support and publicize various types of training opportunities available to participants in the church's training program. These training opportunities include those conducted by associational leaders, state convention leaders, and Southern Baptist Convention leaders.

The director of church training should be aware of the various promotional items available, and should request these items in sufficient quantities for use in his church. The majority of such promotional materials are free upon request from the respective state convention Church Training office. Other materials are supplied at modest costs.

SPACE

The church building is a resource which vitally affects the church's training program. It is possible, of course, to train with inadequate physical resources. However, this is a handicap which most churches can eliminate.

1. Determining Space Needs

The director is responsible for determining space needed by all units of the training program. These space needs include:

(1) SPACE FOR PLANNING MEETINGS. This should be a room which is available on Sunday evenings, and at other times when needed, for general planning. The room should be large enough to accommodate a planning group of about eight to fifteen people. A room immediately adjacent to the area where records and supplies are kept would be convenient. This arrangement would make needed

information readily available to planning groups when necessary.

Other program organizations could use this room at times appropriate to their program needs. Scheduling the use of the room could be done by an assigned person—church secretary, minister of education, pastor, or some lay person specially designated. A form could be used for requesting the room, or a bulletin board or chalkboard in a hallway may be used for this purpose.

(2) SPACE FOR TRAINING SUPPLIES AND MATERIALS. Perhaps this space will need to be shared with other church program organizations. Space for completing records and for dispensing supplies may consist of a room with a desk (with drawers) or a table (with filing space in cabinets or closets). In a church with more adequate finances and more commodious building appointments, space would likely take on greater proportions, such as: separate closets, filing space, supplies distribution areas, records desks and tables.

Church training leaders should recommend to the church that space assigned to them be labeled to identify it as pertaining to the training program. Other church program leaders would need to make a similar recommendation regarding space assigned to them. This would eliminate frustration and inefficiency in handling and dispensing records and supplies.

(3) SPACE FOR ASSEMBLING LARGER GROUPS TO COMMUNICATE GENERAL CHURCH TRAINING INFORMATION. The church auditorium, church fellowship hall, or some other large space may be used periodically for assembling all leaders and members (Youth and Adults). Perhaps this need would occur more often in the non-departmentized church training program, but it may also occur in the larger church training programs.

(4) SPACE FOR PERSONS MOVING TO AND FROM TRAINING SESSIONS. Church training leaders should join with leaders of other church programs in recommending wide corridors and hallways throughout church buildings.

(5) SPACE FOR RECREATION AND DRAMA ACTIVITIES. These activities enhance the spirit of fellowship as well as being a vital part of Christian training. Space for these activities can be shared jointly by all program organizations.

2. Providing Space Needed

Church building survey and planning groups should provide adequately for space needed to conduct the church training program. Church training leaders should submit proposals to the church building planning group showing the amount, types, specifications, etc., of the space needed by the church training program. Such survey and planning should be done prior to construction of new buildings or remodeling of existing buildings.

Church training leaders should follow any established procedures the church may have for submitting space requests and recommendations.

3. Inventorying Space Needs

A periodic checkup should be made to ascertain space needs. Such a checkup will provide the information that leaders will need as they submit proposals and recommendations noted in the two preceding paragraphs.

4. Maintaining Space Needed

Maintenance of space is the responsibility of the church property and custodial committees. However, church training leaders should be alert to any maintenance problems or needs and should report these immediately to proper committee chairmen.

EQUIPMENT

1. Determining Equipment Needs

In a room where planning meetings are held, equipment should include chairs, tables, an easel, and a chalkboard. Leaders of church training should request the amount and types of equipment needed when scheduling a planning meeting.

Equipment needed in areas where training records and supplies are used and dispensed includes items such as desks, tables, cabinets for both filing and storage, an adding machine, and a typewriter.

The amount and types of equipment needed by general officers of Training Union will be determined by several factors. These factors include available finances, volume of records and supplies to be used and dispensed, types of meetings to be held for general officers, and total space available to all church programs and services.

The furnishings for Training Union space should be consistent with those desired by other programs. Sizes, types, etc., have been standardized. Any difference should be in use, quantity, and arrangement.

2. Providing Equipment Needed

Since certain equipment will need to be shared with other program organizations in many churches, Training Union leaders should request that appropriate labels be prepared to identify those items of equipment specifically assigned to the church training program. The Training Union director, in consultation with other general officers, should request additional equipment whenever it is needed in order to increase the efficiency of operation of the church training program.

3. Inventory of Equipment Needs

Much of the equipment provided for general officers in the church training program will be equipment used at other times by other church programs and services. Therefore, an inventory of such equipment is the responsibility of the church committee so assigned. Training Union leaders should assist this committee in securing and maintaining an inventory of equipment.

4. Maintenance of Equipment

Training Union leaders should watch for needed repairs and servicing of equipment used in the church's training program. Needed maintenance should be reported to the appropriate person or committee so that it may be accomplished.

Occasionally the training program will have need for special equipment. When such equipment is bought, it should become the property of the church and should be available for general use.

FINANCES

Financial resources are the monetary resources required to carry out the activities of an organization. Financial resources for the church training program should be provided by the church in keeping with and controlled by church policies and procedures concerning money. It is a common practice among churches to operate on the basis of an annual budget. In order for the church training program to be adequately provided for, the Training Union director and his workers should develop and submit to church budget planners a summary of financial needs. When financial resources have been allocated by the church to the training program, it is the responsibility of church training leaders to use the resources as designated and to follow all church policies and procedures with reference to money.

Leaders should encourage members of respective training units to participate in church decisions concerning the budget, and in subscribing the budget through regular tithes and offerings. Opportunity should be given, particularly in the Youth and the Adult divisions, for interpretation and discussion of a proposed budget. Members of training units should be encouraged to tithe their income in order that the adopted budget may be met.

Th purpose of this section is to describe what church training leaders need to know and to do about determining financial needs and about procuring, using, and accounting for financial resources.

1. Determining Financial Needs

Training needs will vary each year. Therefore, church training leaders should present budget needs at least annually so that overall church budget planning may be intelligently done. Leaders of church training would do well, however, to anticipate budget needs for more than one year at a time. Long-range (three to five years) budget needs should be made known to church stewardship committees. This will enable church budget planning to provide for anticipated growth and enlargement.

Before financial needs for a given period can be determined, other aspects of planning the church training program for the period should have been tentatively completed. The extent of the program, the organization, and the physical resources need to be known as a basis for determining financial needs. These plans should be developed as outlined in chapter 5. With these plans in hand, the Training Union director should guide the leaders of departments and groups to analyze the plans for the purpose of estimating costs. Items such as the following should be considered:

(1) TRAINING MATERIALS

Literature	Record supplies
Curriculum supplements	Other
Special study materials	

(2) ADDITIONAL EQUIPMENT

Chairs	Easel
Tables	Audiovisuals
Chalkboard	Other

(3) ACTIVITIES/PROJECTS

Socials, fellowships, etc.	Assistance for persons
Meals at planning meetings	participating in sem-
Training school for leaders	inars, institutes, etc.
Assistance for persons attending	Other activities
state or SBC assemblies	

2. Procuring Financial Resources

Financial resources for the church training program should be supplied from the general church treasury as authorized by the church budget (or financial plan).

Of necessity, church stewardship committees work on the church's total budget well in advance of the annual budget promotion. In order for this committee to plan the budget intelligently, program leaders must determine their respective budget needs and present these needs to the church budget committee.

The director of church training should submit budget requests annually to the church stewardship committee. Budget requests should include provision for all financial needs identified in the preceding section "Determining Financial Needs." The budget should include requests from the various departments and training groups of the church's training program.

The church training director should base all budget requests upon training to be provided and activities to be performed. Priorities should be determined by the church training council. These priorities should be considered as budget requests and presented to the church's budget-planning group.

The church training director should be able to interpret and justify each item in his budget request. He can present a stronger case to the budget-planning group if his budget request consists of program *needs* and not just program *wants*. He will not necessarily include every detail and every itemized expenditure anticipated by departments and training groups. Instead, he should organize his budget request around the following three categories: Training Materials, Additional Equipment, and Activities/Projects.

The church training director should schedule a deadline date when budget requests from departments and training groups should be submitted to him. He should study these various requests with members of the church training council to determine priority needs and necessary adjustments. He should then submit to the church stewardship committee the total budget needed by the church's training program for the next fiscal period.

When a proposed budget has been adopted by the church, leaders in departments and training groups should accept a continuing responsibility to see that the budget is subscribed and met. Periodic references to the budget, the status of gifts, and the matter of a surplus or a deficit, should be made in department and training group meetings.

Should there be a deficit in the church's budget requiring a cutback in funds, church training leaders should be willing to accept their proportionate share of the reduction of funds.

Needs and circumstances change during a church year, and it is not always possible to anticipate these changes. Therefore, the church training director should be permitted during the year to request necessary adjustments and/or transfers in financial resources. For example, if an enlistment campaign is more successful than anticipated, the cost of additional literature and supplies may exceed the budget estimate.

3. Using Financial Resources

All church training leaders should assume personal responsibility for using wisely the funds allocated for their area of work. They should make every attempt to stay within budget amounts. When new programs or unanticipated needs develop after funds have been allocated, church training leaders should be quick to determine the extent of the additional needs and submit supplementary budget requests.

All church training officers are expected to operate within church policies and procedures concerning the use of money. The director should become informed about the policies, procedures, and forms which the church uses and communicate this information to his workers. The policies and procedures may involve the use of check requisitions, petty cash, purchase orders, etc. All church training leaders should cooperate wholeheartedly with the church's plans for handling money and should urge those who work with them to do so.

If a church does not have policies and procedures for using money, the director of church training and his co-workers should encourage the church to adopt a system of operation in this important area. Until the church establishes such policies and procedures, the director is free to follow his own judgment in working out approaches to be used within the church training program.

4. Accounting for Financial Resources

Leaders should give an accurate accounting of church money allocated to their work. The church training director should make available to leaders any forms which the church has prepared and encourage the leaders to use them. Every leader is responsible for communicating this information as needed to those who work under his guidance.

SUMMARY

1. Physical resources a training program needs include space, equipment, and supplies.
2. Curriculum materials are tools, or resources, for leaders and learners to use in stimulating and guiding learning activities and experiences.
3. New curriculum materials are available for all age groups in the church training program.
4. The New Church Study Course provides additional training resources for members and leaders.
5. The magazine which replaces *The Baptist Training Union Magazine* is *Church Training*.
6. Curriculum outlines for each year are published in the May issue of *Church Training*.
7. Undated units, resource units, and other material of permanent nature should be cataloged and stored in the church library.
8. Training needs should be carefully considered when churches consider building or remodeling.

Chapter Five

THE CHURCH TRAINING PROGRAM
IN ACTION

IF THE CHURCH TRAINING PROGRAM serves the churches adequately, its leaders must give serious attention to planning.

Planning is not optional; it is basic. Planning must be done regularly, adequately, and systematically if the church training program is to achieve its goals. Planning insures success, guarantees good training sessions, and contributes to good esprit de corps among leaders. Planning gives leaders a sense of security and accomplishment. Thus, planning reduces resignations, prevents leadership failures, and makes excellent leaders of ordinary leaders.

Effective planning is forward-looking and aims at preventing problems before they occur. Leaders need to recognize several types of planning: goal planning, process planning, activity planning, project planning, and calendar planning. Leaders need to recognize that planning may be done in many ways and at various times.

Planning for the church training program should be done in the context of the total church planning process. All programs and services in a church should coordinate their planning in connection with the "Program Planning, Leadership Training, and Church Program

Launching Plan." (See Appendix II for detailed description.) This plan is designated to provide guidance for churches in scheduling planning and training activities in connection with the beginning of each church year.

WHAT TO PLAN

The church training director should accept the responsibility for annual planning. Some planning occurs in the church council. The director may suggest training program goals and actions to the church council and work out the schedules for such activities as they relate to the annual church schedule of activities. In the church council, the director can get counsel from other church program leaders and can assist them in their training needs.

In planning the total church training program, the director of church training should accept responsibility for the following administrative planning actions:

1. Establish objectives and goals

2. Determine priorities

3. Plan actions

4. Set up organization

5. Enlist and train personnel

6. Assign and define responsibilities

7. Allocate resources

8. Maintain communications

9. Evaluate results

The director of church training may choose to use cycle planning. If he is a new director, he should begin with step 1 in the cycle. If he has had previous experience, he should start with step 9 (evaluation) and build on the results of his evaluation.

The cycle of administrative planning may be charted as follows:

CYCLE PLANNING

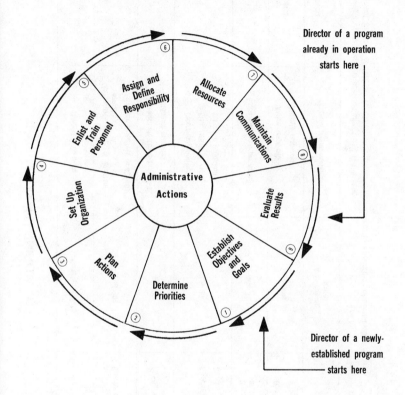

The director may prefer to take a linear approach rather than a cycle approach to his responsibility of planning the total church training program. A checklist for linear planning may include the following items:

LINEAR PLANNING

Date for Beginning	Thing(s) to Be Done	Completion Date	Person(s) or Group Responsible
March or June	Evaluate results of program in operation*	April 30	Director and Training Union council
April 1	Establish objectives and goals** Determine priorities	May 1	Director and Training Union council
May 1	Plan actions Set up organization	May 20	Director and Training Union council Director
May 1	Enlist and train personnel	June 31	Director, with assistance from pastor or other staff members
September 1	Assign responsibility Allocate resources	September 20	Director Director and general secretary
A continuing action	Maintain communications	A continuing action	Director

*Director for a training program already in operation should start at this point.

**After actions suggested for March or June are completed, other sequential actions may be combined on whatever basis is needed.

The linear chart is based on the assumption that the church will elect or reelect the director by April. The chart suggests beginning and completion dates for types of planning and may serve as a check-list for the director.

WHO SHOULD PLAN

The church council and church training council are the chief planning bodies of the church training program.

The church training council is made up of all officers who are responsible for the church training program. These officers include:

1. The director, who serves as chairman of the council
2. All other general officers, such as director of enlistment and general secretary
3. The directors of the three types of training—director of new church member orientation, director of church member train-ing, and director of church leader training
4. The age-group coordinators for churches that have such offi-cers, and
5. The pastor and other appropriate staff members

The churches that have only a church member training program will include the age-group department or training group leaders in the church training council.

HOW TO PLAN

The linear-planning chart, showing beginning and completion dates, is designed to stress steps of planning prior to the beginning of a church year. Actually, planning should take place throughout the year. The Training Union council acts as a coordinating group. It assigns special projects to appropriate departments and training groups and plans training opportunities for workers.

The following suggested agenda for a Training Union council offers some help in how to plan:

1. Scripture reading and prayer
2. Roll call

3. Evaluation, study of records, reports, etc. (The council should ask such questions as: What have we accomplished? What are we doing? How well are we doing?)
4. Determination of needs, problems, goals, etc. (Ask, What do we need to do?)
5. Assignment of responsibility in writing (Who is going to do these things?)
6. Schedules, dates, deadlines, etc. (When are these things to be completed?)
7. Adjourn

The director of church training needs to take ideas and tentative plans—involving council members in all possible ways—to the council meeting. The secret of successful planning is for the plans to become the concern of all members in the planning group.

The director should be acquainted with and make available the tools to help in planning for and conducting the church training program. These tools will include:

1. Attendance records system
2. Reports of work done
3. *Church Training Resources and Planning Guide*
4. *New Church Member Orientation Manual* (*Revised*)
5. *Handbook for Director of Leader Training*
6. Denominational calendar
7. Church calendar
8. *Sourcebook 70–71*
9. *Church Planning Guide*
10. Visitation prospect list
11. *Church Training*
12. Periodical materials
13. Other resources material

WHEN TO PLAN

The director of church training should do much individual planning in preparation for group planning. His planning should be tentative and flexible in order to adjust to the ideas of others. He should seek various opportunities to plan with small groups or individuals. Some planning can be done by telephone, during coffee breaks and luncheons, in church corridors before and after church meetings, or in homes.

The church training council meeting provides a good opportunity for group planning. Church training councils should meet at least once each month on a date and at an hour *regularly scheduled* in the church calendar. Additional meetings may be scheduled as needed.

The exact date for the church training council to meet depends somewhat on the schedule for other meetings, such as the church council meeting and planning group meetings. All planning meetings should be coordinated so that appropriate information and recommendations can be presented to the church council.

Council meetings may be conducted on any day of the week. When only general officers and directors serve on the council, the Sunday evening training hour may be used.

The length of time the council meets is important. If the council meets monthly, at least one hour would be needed.

Consideration has been given to planning by the church training director and other general officers. However, the director has a responsibility for administering planning in all department, and training groups. There are two possible approaches in the discharge of this responsibility.

First, the director may establish a general monthly planning meeting in the church calendar. Every church needs to determine the best time for this meeting. Some churches designate one Wednesday night for this type of planning; others use Sunday afternoons.

All group, department, and general officers should be invited. The meeting could start with a meal and a general period for announcements, general reports and promotion, and inspiration. Large or small group planning sessions could follow, depending on organizational requirements of the training program. Discussion of planning for departments and training groups can be found in other chapters of this book and in manuals for the age divisions.

A second approach to general planning is to allow every unit of the organization to schedule and conduct planning sessions at the convenience of leaders and members. This flexible approach may be the only workable plan in some churches. To insure success with this approach, the director will need to promote the idea vigorously, encourage leaders, provide assistance when problems arise, and ask for reports in council meetings.

HOW TO CARRY OUT THE PLANS

The first step in implementing plans is communicating quickly and clearly with those responsible for the work that is planned. The nature and complexity of the communication will determine how it should be approached. The director of church training should see that all persons involved and affected by the project or action are properly informed. If a study course is planned, it should be cleared with the church council. If extra funds are required, the finance committee should be consulted. If a church meal is involved, the church hostess should be consulted.

The type of action planned will determine how much and what type of promotion is needed. Many actions will require skilful interpretation and promotion in the church. Such events as associational or church leadership schools, enlargement or visitation efforts, short-term training projects for parents of teenagers, awards banquets, or an associational "M" night require promotion. The church training council should decide what promotion is needed and how it will be done. Good promotion often involves announcements, letters, telephone calls, posters, enlistment and training of leaders, preparation of visitation cards, ordering literature, checking with the church library, and attending to many other details. The mark of good planning is the ability to foresee the details needed to make a plan work. The mark of good administration is the ability to delegate responsibility.

Another principle related to effective administration is delegation of responsibility through leaders. If, for example, the project planned is a visitation emphasis to add fifty new members, then the director of enlistment should be given the assignment and should be allowed to direct it. He should see that prospect cards are made, people are enlisted to visit, goals are set, and all other arrangements are made.

The director of church training should delegate responsibility, expect the job to be done, and give proper recognition when completed.

The director of church training and other leaders in the organization should expect and receive reports on assignments made by them. Plans for reporting should be built into the assignment. The worker should know what he is to report and why the report is needed.

A final principle in administrative planning is the proper recognition of the persons responsible for the work. Merited recognition builds morale, provides motivation, and paves the way for better work. Recognition may be a simple personal and private expression of honest appreciation. Recognition may be a letter or telephone call. Recognition may be given in the church training council, before the church, through the church bulletin, or in some other public manner. The director will succeed to the degree that he builds a corps of dedicated, committed workers. Genuine appreciation and recognition constitute one way of accomplishing this.

In summary, these are the essentials for putting plans into actions:

- Communicate assignments clearly
- Interpret and promote vigorously
- Delegate responsibility
- Expect and receive reports on assignments
- Make appropriate recognition of work done

An old axiom is that leaders may not accomplish all they plan, but they are sure to accomplish no more than they plan. Thus, planning is not optional; it is imperative. Planning is essential. Planning is the road to a better church training program. Planning is the key to better programs, to learning, to Christian growth, to skill development, to knowledge, to changed attitudes, and to changed church members.

SUMMARY

1. Planning is not optional; it is basic.
2. Planning gives leaders a sense of security and accomplishment.
3. The church council and the training program council are the chief planning bodies of the church training program.

4. The church training council is made up of the general officers of the training program, plus department directors in some churches.
5. The director of church training should be acquainted with all needed materials for planning and conducting the church training program.
6. The training program council should meet at least once each month on a date and hour scheduled in the church council.
7. The first step in implementing good plans is communicating quickly and clearly with those persons responsible for the work planned.
8. Persons who perform jobs should receive proper recognition from the director of church training.

Chapter Six

CHURCH TRAINING
IMPROVEMENT

HAS THIS ever happened to you? You made extensive plans for some event. When the event was over, you did not take time to write down the strengths and weaknesses of the occasion or to list ways it could be improved. To make matters worse, you later find yourself on a committee to repeat the event you had previously planned and find your memory "playing tricks" on you. You cannot remember what it was that made you say, "I'll not make that mistake again!" This can happen—and does happen again and again—when all the effort goes into planning and none into analyzing the results for positive and negative values.

What we are talking about is called evaluation. D. Campbell Wyckoff defines evaluation as "a process of comparing what is with what ought to be, in order to determine areas and directions for improvement." [1] Evaluation is making judgments about what has happened or about the worth of something. LeRoy Ford has called evaluation a "stock-take." Evaluation helps us to know where we are going and

---

1. From *How to Evaluate Your Christian Education Program* by D. Campbell Wyckoff. Copyright © 1962 by W. L. Jenkins. The Westminster Press. Used by permission.

how far we have progressed. In church training, evaluation is determining the degree to which a goal or aim has been achieved. The aims or goals serve as points of reference. The evaluation may be as specific as the aim or goal. We must know what results are desired before we can determine to what degree they have been achieved.

WHAT TO EVALUATE

The results of a church training program in operation need evaluation. This is the starting point for a training program already established. An evaluation of the program will help to establish goals for the continuing program. The reverse is true of a church beginning a program. The goals for church training come from a church's determining its training needs. These needs are based upon desired church goals. Evaluation tests the results of the program.

There are two types of evaluation of a church training program. The first type is process evaluation. This pertains to enlistment, organization, activities, methods, materials, equipment, and other resources. The other type is product evaluation. It has to do with results in the lives of the participants. Product evaluation is concerned with what knowledge, attitudes and skills a person has developed, and how well the person is functioning as a genuine Christian and how meaningfully involved he has become in the covenant relationship and in the life and work of the church.

The evaluation of process is of value because it helps to improve the results of training.

Proper evaluation of the number of people enlisted and involved in church training is important. If efforts to enlist persons in training are not successful, there will be no "product" of training to evaluate. The answers to the following questions reveal some basis for evaluation:

1. What plans were made for enlisting and involving members in training? Which plans were effective? Which should be continued?
2. What areas of concern were not dealt with this year that need attention? How shall we meet this challenge?

The quality of training is vital to a good church training program. An evaluation should indicate what the member learned and what skills were developed. It will point to materials and processes which provided understanding and growth. It will also bring into focus deficiencies and difficulties that need correction if the quality of training is to be improved.

A major concern of evaluation is to ascertain whether the church training program is doing its part in realizing church goals. This is valid reason for a church to have a training program. Careful testing will indicate strength and weakness at this point. This training will include new member orientation and church leader training as well as member training.

Evaluation should also be concerned with helping a church to learn if the church is meeting the interests of individual members and aiding the members in the development of individual skills. Evaluation is applied on every level: individual member, training group, age-group, department, division, and church program level.

Evaluation should include assembly programs, study selection sessions, materials, learning aids, resources, records, socials, and any other activity or function which make up the training program.

In a departmental or group meeting, evaluation could stimulate these questions:

1. What progress was made toward general training objectives? What progress was made in meeting the needs of the individual?
2. What are some mistakes we have made? What have we learned?
3. What progress have we made in solving problems?

WHO SHOULD EVALUATE?

Since training is a church task, the church itself is responsible for evaluating its church training program. This evaluation begins with individual member self-evaluation. These questions may guide the evaluation:

1. Has training increased my knowledge, understanding, and skills?

2. Have my attitudes become more Christian?
3. Am I better able to function as a Christian and church member?

This type of evaluation may be accomplished by participants engaging in self-evaluation through the use of checklists or questionnaires. These evaluations will reveal different types of information.

Members of units and training groups should evaluate their work. General officers should provide the channels for receiving and considering the group members' evaluations.

Leaders of each type of training—new member, member, and leader—should make evaluation an important part of the weekly and monthly activities.

The church training council has the primary responsibility for evaluating the church's training program. The council should acquire the information required for evaluation. The council should observe, receive reports, make decisions, and interpret the church's training goals to other training leaders. Progress toward the attainment of these goals should be evaluated. The church training council must carefully evaluate the total effectiveness of the church training program.

The director of church training should share the evaluation with the church council regularly for its information and direction. This is done by the director's written report and the recommendations he makes orally or written to the council.

The evaluation process then, in a sense, starts from both ends of the church's training program. Each individual provides evaluation on his level to other responsible people who carry it through the church training council to the church council and on to the church congregation. The more thorough the process of evaluation, the better the trained product will be. The "trained product"—the trained Christian—is the real purpose for a training program.

WAYS TO EVALUATE

When a church begins to evaluate its program, it should ask whether its goals and objectives are understandable. A church may discover that its goals and objectives are not right or proper. Evaluating activities helps to clarify and strengthen training activities. Evaluation should also cause a church to test the effectiveness of its church training program. If people's needs are not being met, the program is ineffective. The church training program must be relevant to the needs of its members and persons in the community.

Not every activity can be measured by numbers. Southern Baptists are learning the value of quality as well as quantity. An evaluation of the quality of training provides knowledge of what is being done and points to what should be done. Quantity is also an important evaluating tool provided it is viewed in the light of quality and relevancy.

In the church training program, "the leader's preparation and leadership are evaluated along with the group's participation in the study and training activities. The methods used and the way they are used, knowledge gained, and attitudes changed are also evaluated." [2] This evaluation can be accomplished by:

1. Self-evaluation by the leader and each group member
2. Oral or written opinions of participants
3. Observation, directed or undirected
4. Tests, oral or written
5. Review charts, checklists, flow charts, or rating charts

To evaluate attendance and involvement in church training one can use:

1. The attendance record system
2. Reports of work done
3. Prospect lists
4. Planned involvement sessions

In the church training council, after receiving reports and viewing the records, these questions may be used to guide the evaluation:

1. What have we accomplished?

---

2. Nora Padgett, "Evaluate the Results," *The Baptist Train Union Magazine,* Feb., 1964, p. 21.

2. What are we doing?
3. How well are we doing?
4. What can we do better?

To evaluate the success of the church's training program in achieving its assigned church goals, it is necessary to ask:

1. Did the program provide the training assigned to it by the church?
2. In what areas did the program excel? Where did it fail?
3. Were the goals challenging enough? Was the plan comprehensive enough? What new emphases are needed to better undergird the church goals?
4. Was a proper balance kept in the new church member, member, and church leader training areas?

In the final analysis of evaluation, the real test of whether the training program is a success or failure is determined by the product it produces. This can be indicated by two words, "commitment" and "involvement."

1. Is there a noticeable difference in the commitment to Christ and the church in those members who have participated in the church training program and those who have not?
2. Do training program members function better in performing the tasks of the church?
3. Do these members give evidence of knowledge in Christian doctrine, ethics, history, church polity and organization?
4. Are training program members meaningfully involved in the life and work of the church in the world?
5. Are these members growing in their leadership potential?

The test of the pudding is in the eating of it! The test of the church training program is in what it produces in the life of an individual for Jesus Christ, his way, and his work!

WHEN TO EVALUATE?

The work of a leader has been called "a glorious cycle. . . . There are three phases in this cycle:

1. Planning
2. Teaching (carrying out your plans)
3. Evaluating

What happens without any one of these phases? . . . If you do not plan, you have no aim. . . . An aim gives direction; and of course, direction shows one where to go. Without this phase of the cycle, frustration may result." [3] "Carrying out the plan" is only as effective as the planning aim. If properly done, the two together result in achievement and growth.

Evaluation, which is the next phase, tests past performance and results. Without it, the next step is difficult indeed because it is phase one all over again—planning. Without all three phases—planning, carrying out the plans, and evaluating—no one phase can be successful. So make the rounds of the cycle regularly. Remember it takes all three!

This cycle must be completed often by the leaders involved in church training. The cycle starts with the director and the church training council. In individual conferences, small groups, chance meetings, and planned meetings, "homework" is done. This work is studied and considered in the church training council for decisions before referral to the church council. The work of a leader is a continuous cycle.

The church training council may meet weekly, monthly, or quarterly as it desires. The important thing is that it must meet to plan and evaluate. Definite times for evaluation must be set aside. Planning meetings for general and departmental officers should include evaluation as a definite part of making plans for the year.

A thorough evaluation should be made as an early part of the process of planning the goals of a church. The results of this evaluation will aid in working out new goals and actions. The director of church training then works with the other church program leaders in the church council in developing goals and actions to recommend to the church. The director of church training not only leads in a

---

3. Kenneth P. Jones, "Planning, Teaching, Evaluating—It Takes All Three," *The Baptist Training Union Magazine,* March, 1969, p. 61.

thorough evaluation of training done the past year, but projects future goals on the basis of this evaluation.

HOW TO TURN EVALUATION INTO IMPROVEMENT

Edward J. Furst said: "Evaluation can serve a variety of purposes, some central and others only peripheral or incidental. The central purposes are to determine the effectiveness of courses and educational programs and to provide a basis for improving them." [4]

Planning is not completed until plans for evaluation are made. Evaluation is of no value unless it leads to improvement. Evaluation shows what has been done. It reviews how it was done. Evaluation reveals what was not done. It points to what can be done in developing a better process to produce a better product. The purpose of evaluation is to bring improvement in process and product:

1. If an evaluation of records shows a steady drop in attendance in an age group, it may indicate that the leadership needs more training or the training sessions need more flexibility or better material.
2. If evaluation of a group indicates a lack of commitment to the church, then steps should be taken both in instruction and involvement to change the picture.
3. If evaluation points to a lack of planning, then the leaders must find a scheduled time and place for planning.
4. If evaluation presents a true picture of a real need for skill in witnessing, then plans should be made for instruction in witnessing. Guided witnessing opportunities should be provided.

The key to evaluation is planning; the key to planning is evaluation. One without the other is not enough. But to stop short of improvement as a result of evaluation is to miss the boat entirely. Experience is still a good teacher. Improvements learned from the experience of evaluation must be built into future plans.

Thus the cycle continues: Plan the work, work the plan, evaluate the results, and improve the plans!

---

4. Edward J. Furst, *Constructing Evaluation Instruments* (New York: David McKay Company, Inc., 1958), p. 4.

SUMMARY

1. Evaluation is "a process of comparing what is with what ought to be, in order to determine areas and direction for improvement."
2. Periodic evaluation of the church training program will help to establish objectives and goals for the program.
3. Good evaluation is of two types, process evaluation and product evaluation.
4. A major concern of evaluation is to determine if the church training program is doing its part in realizing church goals.
5. Since training is a church task, the church itself is responsible for evaluating its church training program.
6. The church training council has the first responsibility for evaluating all aspects of the training program.
7. Evaluation is of little or no value unless it leads to improvement.
8. The key to evaluation is planning and the key to planning is evaluation.

Chapter Seven

NEW CHURCH MEMBER ORIENTATION

JESUS makes it very clear that the call to discipleship is a call to commitment unto him as Saviour and Lord. " 'No one can serve two masters' " (Matt. 6 : 24, NASB).[1] Again he said, " 'Whoever does not carry his own cross and come after Me cannot be My disciple' " (Luke 14 : 27, NASB).

Many modern-day Christians have not realized that commitment means saying no to self and yes to Christ. Commitment is not a matter of "what I want to do" or even "what I ought to do." When one is motivated by love for Jesus Christ and activated by gratitude for him, commitment and obedience follow. The "I want" and "I ought" give way to "I will" and "I can." Real inner peace and joy come as a result of this commitment.

QUEST FOR A COMMITTED CHURCH

"Commitment" is basic to the individual Christian and to the church, if the church is to be and do that which is imperative in our day. "How" to get this commitment is important. Commitment comes from understanding. The deeper the understanding, the

---

1. *New American Standard Bible, New Testament,* © The Lockman Foundation, 1960, 1962, 1963.

deeper the commitment. New church member orientation seeks to provide information for a basic understanding of the meaning of conversion and of the tasks of the church. New member orientation seeks to help new members become committed to the life and work of the church.

"When" is another key word to commitment. Should it be assumed that commitment will automatically come to the new church member? New church member orientation seeks to develop understanding in the new member at the beginning of his church relationship through basic, initial training. As each new church member becomes a committed, involved participant in the life and work of the church, the church itself can become a committed church.

ORGANIZING NEW CHURCH MEMBER ORIENTATION

Training Union implements new member orientation as one of its tasks. The director of church training is responsible for this training. In many churches he will have the total responsibility. In other churches, another general officer may be designated as the director of new member orientation. He would serve under the direction of the director of church training. In some cases, the pastor may assume this responsibility for new member orientation.

The organization for new member orientation requires church-elected leaders with three distinct responsibilities: (1) initial counseling sessions for new members, (2) teaching sessions required by the course of instruction, and (3) a final summary session to encourage the involvement of new members in the life and work of the church.

A small church may assign these three responsibilities to one person. Larger churches with many new members may need a director of new member orientation and a counselor and/or instructor for Adult, Youth, and Children. Some churches will need an orientation secretary; other churches will select and train sponsors to serve.

All leaders need a knowledge of the techniques and concepts of new member orientation as outlined in the *New Church Member Orientation Manual* (*Revised*).

The factors determining the pattern of organization a church should adopt for its new member orientation are: size and location of the church, ages of new members, the number who are new converts and transfers, regularity of additions, available leaders and space, schedule of activities, and the church's attitudes toward orientation.

The number of new members received during the year and the regularity of additions are more important than church size in determining the orientation program which should be established.

In some churches with twenty-five or fewer new members each year, the pastor may choose to assume all the duties for counseling and instructing new members. All new members would meet in one combined class, entering the class as they are received by the church.

The following organization is suggested for churches which have between twenty-five and fifty new members each year: (1) enlarge the new member orientation to two classes, one for Adult-Youth and one for Children; (2) select lay leaders to serve as director, counselor-instructor, and sponsor. The pastor serves in roles of his choice.

The following organization is suggested for churches with more than fifty new members each year: (1) enlarge the number of classes to three, Adult, Youth, and Children, (2) form these classes into a new church orientation training department or assign the classes to the existing age-grade departments, and (3) place emphasis upon more lay leaders as director, counselors, instructors, sponsors, and secretaries. The director of new member orientation would be responsible for leadership. The pastor serves in roles of his choice.

RESOURCES FOR NEW CHURCH MEMBER ORIENTATION

Many new and improved plans for new member orientation are described in the *New Church Member Orientation Manual* (*Revised*). The orientation which it outlines is the result of six years of careful study and research. It reflects the thinking and experience of hundreds of Southern Baptist leaders who contributed to its development. The *New Church Member Orientation Manual* (*Revised*) is listed in the Christian Leadership Courses of the New Church Study Course. The manual is available from Baptist Book Stores.

Six pieces of curriculum material are available for use by the churches in the orientation of new members. These booklets are attractive in format, sound in educational procedures, biblical in foundation, and effective in helping new church members to grow and serve.

Three of these curriculum pieces are designed for use by the new members themselves. They are graded by age levels: Children, Youth, and Adults. For each graded new member's booklet, there is also a teacher's guide. These booklets are undated and may be ordered at any time from the Church Literature Department of the Baptist Sunday School Board. The titles for the guides are: *Promises to Keep* (Older Children), *Belonging* (Youth), and *In Covenant* (Adult). Both the new member's booklet and the teacher's guide for counselors and teachers follow a similar pattern. Each contains thirteen chapters. The content includes the following subjects: "The Meaning of Conversion" and "The Meaning of Church Membership." These two chapters are to be used for the counseling sessions.

The following chapters are for the instruction sessions: "Your New Life in Christ," "Your Growth as a Christian," "Your Bible and Its Use," "Your Church and Its Covenant," "Your Church and Its Beliefs," "Your Church Working Together," "Your Church Working with Others," "Your Church and Its History," "Your Church and Your Home," and "Sharing Your Faith."

A summary session concludes the orientation. Suggestions for this session are found in each booklet. This summary session is designed to give opportunity for questions and unresolved problems and to enlist the new members in further training.

A church can conduct thirteen sessions using one chapter for each session. Or, certain chapters may be combined if fewer sessions are desired. Churches may use all the chapters to provide training for new converts and use selected chapters for the transfer members.

A church will need to prepare copies of its church covenant, articles of faith, church history, budget, and other necessary local items for use during the sessions.

To record the attendance of new members, a "New Church Member Attendance Record" is available from the Baptist Book Stores. It is recommended for use as a part of the church's training records and may be a personal record for teachers and instructors of new members.

A "New Member Certificate" is also available from the Baptist Book Stores to be given to new members upon completion of the orientation. A church may use the certificate to publicly recognize all those members who complete orientation. This recognition helps to keep the importance of new member training before the church.

Because of the importance of new members, their training needs should be high on the church's list of space priorities.

Counseling sessions should be conducted in a room which is private and quiet. There should be no interruption or interference during this important discussion. The same facility may be used for the summary session.

Room requirements for instruction sessions would be similar to those of any other group of comparable size and age. If the training is done in a combined class for all ages, a room planned for about twenty people would be needed. If the room is too large, the spirit of participation may be affected.

If two or more new member classes meet at the same time, a department room and adjacent classrooms are needed. This would also be true if the classes function as a department and meet together as an assembly for special features. If the classes meet at different times, the same room could be used for all the classes.

Storage space should be provided either in the training area, church library, or some other space suitable for keeping supplies and materials.

Rooms for new member orientation should be properly equipped and furnished for effective age-group learning experiences. Furnishings and equipment for the rooms should include tackboard, chalkboard, supply closet or cabinet, and a hanging device for projection screen.

Furnishings should include an adequate number of proper-size chairs arranged to contribute to a good learning situation. Tables should be available as needed for workgroup activities. Devices for darkening the windows are recommended.

Most of the equipment and furnishings needed for new member

training will already be in the department or classroom and will be used by other programs of the church.

The use of audiovisuals and other equipment needed for special training activities should be scheduled in advance. It is important to have a "trial run" to be sure that everything is working properly beforehand.

Financial resources for new member orientation should be provided through the church budget. Leaders should analyze their financial needs and give this information to the director of new member orientation. He, in turn, will use the information given to him by his workers in helping to determine the total budget for the training program. This information would be shared with the director of church training and the Training Union council.

PLANNING AND CONDUCTING NEW CHURCH MEMBER ORIENTATION

The director of new member orientation is responsible for planning and conducting the new member training. He works closely with the director of church training. He serves on the church training council where he coordinates new member orientation with other aspects of the training program. (For a fuller listing of the responsibilities of the director of new member orientation, see chapter 3.) If church training does not have a director of new member orientation, the church training director is responsible for planning the training for new church members.

The director of new member orientation should develop and present plans to the director of church training and the church training council. Planning should include time and schedule of meetings, type of class or classes offered, method of enlisting and training leadership, budget needs, location of classes, ways to enlist new members in new member training, and other necessary items.

A monthly or quarterly meeting of the new member orientation leadership should be held to plan, promote, and evaluate the orientation.

The planning process begins with a church's decision to provide orientation for new church members. According to the church's policy, the schedule and procedure for new member training are planned. This results in the election of the person responsible for new member orientation and provides guidelines for planning and conducting the training.

IMPROVING NEW MEMBER ORIENTATION

The content and activities provided in the *New Church Member Orientation Manual* (*Revised*) and the graded materials for teachers and members will serve as the basis of the program.

The approach a church makes to new member orientation must be realistic and flexible. A church must have new members to have new member orientation. The larger the number of new members available, the more the program must be expanded. Also, the regularity of new additions determines whether the training should be continuous, occasional, or annual. However, the important thing is to provide training for each new member. A very small class may well be the best class. An informal, personal atmosphere will contribute to better orientation.

Guidelines for organization, based upon number and regularity of additions, can be found under "Organizing New Church Member Orientation" in this chapter.

The following suggestions should assist churches in tailoring new member orientation to meet the needs of transfer members:

1. The counseling session is recommended for all transfer members. Rather than using the approach suggested for the new convert, it may be better to ask transfer members to share their testimony of conversion and church experience.
2. Transfer members include persons of widely varied backgrounds. The degree to which the following factors are dealt with will affect the adequacy of new member orientation and the ease of enlisting new members in it. The factors are: previous training, Christian maturity, meaningful church membership, religious background, church service record, physical conditions, personal problems, inability to attend orientation, and permanency of residence.

3. For transfer members, the following topics of instruction may be sufficient: "Your Church and Its Covenant," "Your Church and Its Beliefs," "Your Church Working Together," "Your Church Working with Others," and "Your Church and Its History." Since these topics follow each other in the cycle of lessons, it might be well to urge each transfer member to attend these sessions and invite him to attend any others which he feels will be of value to him.

The following suggestions are simple approaches to new member orientation designed to assist small churches in providing improved training—graded to some extent.

By using the same person to work with different age groups and by providing a different time schedule for age-grade classes, it is possible for a church with limited leadership to provide graded new member orientation. A new member class could be conducted on Sunday morning for Adults and Youth. A class for Children could be held on Sunday evening. One leader could conduct all of the classes.

Most churches will want to make extensive use of sponsors in helping new members become involved in the fellowship and work of the church. Sponsors are recommended to serve as Christian friends to new members. They may serve as individual or family sponsors. Although deacons often make excellent sponsors, the work should not be confined to them. Mature youth and women often have the unique abilities to be good sponsors. Senior citizens have the experience, interest, and time to make excellent sponsors. The sponsorship is usually for the duration of the new member orientation sessions.

The new member orientation in many churches can be strengthened through greater emphasis upon the place of the testimony in the counseling session.

Unless a Christian is able to give his testimony to fellow believers, it is doubtful that he will be able to share it with unbelievers. If necessary, the counselor should help each new member prepare his testimony and encourage him to share it. Accompanied by a seasoned Christian, the new member should be given the privilege of sharing in witnessing experiences where he can become involved.

Many churches need to make better use of the final new member orientation summary session. The more private and personal the summary session, the more the new member will benefit from it. Perhaps, the person who counsels the new member should lead this session. If he is someone other than the pastor, it may be helpful to involve the pastor also. Sufficient time for review and evaluation is important. The new member should receive answers to questions and guidance for the future as he continues to train for further growth and service.

Churches will need continued emphasis on enlisting new members in training.

Although orientation of new members is a task assigned to the church training program, the church must share a conviction that it is vital to the well-being of the total church. New member orientation seeks a regenerated, committed, and involved Christian and church member from the very beginning of the new member's life in Christ and the church. New member orientation deserves such a priority that a church should state its policies on new member training.

Every church should feel that this orientation helps the church express its ministry of love and concern to each new member. This will mean that new member orientation will not be an optional matter for a church or the new member. A church should feel that it is obligated to provide this training for each new member. The new member deserves to be so counseled and instructed that he can verify his conversion and receive understanding for commitment and involvement in the life and work of the church in the world.

Yes, the church should provide orientation for each new member. The church should determine its policy for new member training so that each new member may receive that which he rightfully deserves.

If new member orientation is to be constantly improved, a church must evaluate its ministry to new members regularly and carefully. The results of the orientation in the lives of new members will indicate points of weakness and strength. This evaluation is an example of product evaluation discussed in chapter 6. The influence of orientation on the lives of new members is the most important test.

In process evaluation, the second type of evaluation described in chapter 6, the focus is on the process by which the results are accomplished. This pertains to the foundation, structure, and scope of new member orientation.

This evaluation should be done by the new member orientation leadership, the church training council, church council, deacons, and in a special sense by the whole church. Expressions of value from those who have received the training will also be beneficial.

To keep improving new member orientation, it is necessary to profit from the evaluation by making necessary changes and by improving the level of leadership commitment, skill, and morale.

REACHING NEW CHURCH MEMBERS FOR TRAINING

Bill Pogue, an astronaut by profession, serves as a director of youth in the training program of his church. In a conversation with this writer, he said: "It is a great day when Baptists realize the need of basic, continuing, and specialized training. Industry realized this a long time ago. It is time for the church to realize it also!" This basic training is new church member orientation. For the new convert, this training provides a spiritual nursery where, as a babe in Christ, he can receive the milk of the Word and be nurtured in a way that will help him to grow and to serve. For the transfer member, this training provides an opportunity for him to verify his Christian experience and receive inspiration and knowledge about the church he has joined. For both the new convert and the transfer member, the church is providing a ministry of love and fellowship which is needed and deserved. For a church, new member training helps to preserve its strength and purity by ministering wisely to its new members.

To reach members for new member orientation, a church must be aware of its own record of member involvement and commitment. The pastor, deacons, and church council can become aware of the need for better new member training by studying the church roll of new members for the past few years. This awareness should bring a desire to improve the situation.

If the pastor, deacons, and church council will study the *New Church Member Orientation Manual (Revised)*, they should be able to develop a plan to aid in solving new member orientation problems. This plan should include these steps:

1. Review or adopt a church covenant, articles of faith, and local church history. The pastor could create an awareness of the problems involved and stimulate thinking toward solutions by preaching and teaching on subjects related to better new member orientation.
2. Secure new member orientation materials.
3. Orient the present membership, if needed. Sufficient time should be allowed for promotion to assure good attendance. The sessions could be held simultaneously for older children, youth, and adults. The sessions may be scheduled during the regular church training or Bible teaching time. Secure enough materials for training sessions for new member orientation leaders.
4. Select, elect, and train leaders.
5. Adopt a church policy on new member orientation.
6. Set up organization and schedule for new member orientation.
7. Assign rooms and equipment.
8. Undergird each step, praying for direction of Holy Spirit.

An enthusiastic adult who completed the new member orientation declared, "Since I came from another denomination, I had a lot of wrong concepts about Baptists. These false concepts were corrected. The orientation materials are tremendous!"

A minister of education commented, "This is the type of instruction which new members have needed for years. No longer is there any excuse for a church member to say he has not had the opportunity to know what is involved in church membership."

An excited senior citizen said: "Now I know what it means to be a Christian and a Baptist. Since I know, I can tell others."

New church member orientation can provide the front door for a covenant relationship, commitment, and discipline. If the front door of training is adequate, perhaps it will eliminate the problem of the back door through which members have been lost from active, spiritual, loving fellowship in Jesus Christ.

SUMMARY

1. Jesus makes it clear that the call to be a disciple is a call to commitment unto him as Saviour and Lord.
2. Commitment comes from understanding.
3. A church has a responsibility to offer training for all its new members.
4. The primary resource for planning and conducting a new member orientation program is the *New Church Member Orientation Manual (Revised)*.
5. The kind of organization a church needs for new member training is primarily determined by the number of members joining the church.
6. Curriculum materials are available for Adults, Youth and Children in new member orientation.
7. Special records are available for use in new member orientation.
8. Sponsors are recommended to serve as Christian friends to new members.
9. For all new members the church provides a ministry of love and understanding through new member orientation.

Chapter Eight

CHURCH MEMBER TRAINING

EVERY CHURCH MEMBER should be trained "for the work of Christian service, to build up the body of Christ" (Eph. 4:12, TEV).[1] The primary constituency of church training is church members. In addition to church members, church training seeks to provide learning experiences for Preschool and Children's groups (ages birth through eleven). The need for all church members to be trained for effective participation and service grows out of the nature and purpose of a New Testament church. Every member is to be a functioning part of the body of Christ.

QUEST FOR A DYNAMIC CHURCH

Church member training may be described as training provided to equip members to participate meaningfully in the life and work of the church in the world.

Member training involves carrying out two training program tasks. These tasks are distinctive.

1. From *Good News for Modern Man, The New Testament in Today's English Version,* © copyright American Bible Society, 1966. Used by permission.

1. *Train Church Members to Perform the Functions of the Church*

This means to help members develop skills to perform the functions of a church: worship, witness, educate, minister, and apply. The foundations for the accomplishment are built into curriculum study areas provided by the church training program.

2. *Teach Christian theology, Christian ethics, Christian history, and church polity and organization*

Through the church training program, learners are involved in meaningful exploration of the realities of the Christian faith and life.

ORGANIZING MEMBER TRAINING

Organization should provide a way to move toward implementing the tasks of church member training. Simplicity, flexibility, and clearly defined responsibility are desirable qualities to maintain in organizational patterns.

1. *Factors Which Influence Organization Are:*

(1) Availability of leadership
(2) Availability of space
(3) Total number of possibilities in each age span
(4) Number of persons in each age division
(5) Special needs of the church
(6) Interests and abilities of members

Each church should analyze its training needs and determine the amount of organization required. Several patterns of organization are suggested which can help a church in setting up its church member training organization.

2. *Patterns of Organization*

(1) Pattern 1

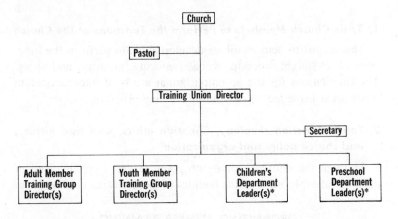

Pattern 1 presents a simplified approach to member training. A church can use this pattern to organize two or three training groups for Adults and a like number for Youth without needing a department organization for either of these age groups. Multiple Children's and Preschool departments are also possible.

(2) Pattern 2

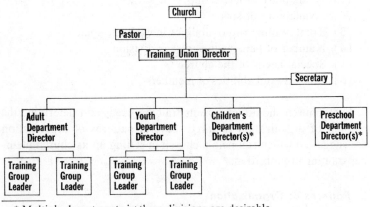

* Multiple departments in these divisions are desirable.

Pattern 2 provides for departments for each age group. Churches using this pattern may organize additional age-group departments as needed.

(3) Pattern 3

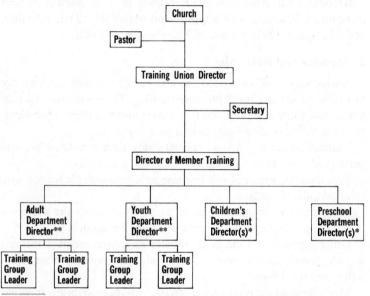

* Multiple departments for these divisions are desirable.
** Multiple departments in these divisions may be needed.

Many churches choose to follow pattern 3. This pattern adds a director of member training, thus relieving the church training director of a number of responsibilities relating to member training.

3. Duties of Director of Church Member Training

The director of church member training is responsible to the church training director for planning, conducting, and evaluating member training for the church. He works closely with the church training director. He serves on the church training council where he coordinates member training with other aspects of the training program. The duties of the director of church member training are listed in chapter 3. If there is no director of church member training, these duties should be performed by the church training director.

RESOURCES FOR MEMBER TRAINING

Resources for church member training may be classified under three major headings: (1) Supplies and Materials, (2) Leadership, and (3) Space. Each of these will be considered briefly.

1. Supplies and Materials

A wide variety of both dated and undated curriculum materials are available for use in church member training. These materials include materials specifically prepared for leaders and members. (See chapter 4 for listing of dated curriculum pieces.)

Undated materials include special study items, undated units in periodicals, and New Church Study Course materials.

Supplemental material and learning aids are available for use with selected units of study.

The variety of materials enable churches to select the materials best fitted to accomplish the particular training needed.

Other supplies and materials for use in church member training include record forms, promotional materials, posters, films, filmstrips, and recordings.

Miscellaneous supplies such as chalk, erasers, newsprint, sentence strip roll, felt pens, thumbtacks, masking tape, Plasti-Tak, pencils, scissors, paste, and brushes should be provided as needed.

2. Leadership

The director of church member training will keep places of leadership filled with the best leaders possible. Workers should meet qualifications for positions held and have prior training in their duties whenever possible.

3. Space

Normally, a church will use for its training program the same areas and equipment which are used by corresponding age groups on Sunday morning.

PLANNING AND CONDUCTING MEMBER TRAINING

The director of church member training is responsible for planning the training opportunities which are available to church members and their families.

Two types of member training need to be planned: (1) that which is done on a continuing basis, and (2) that which is done in short-term projects.

All plans should be presented to the church training council. The council includes all church training department directors (or, in nondepartment organizations, the group leaders).

The church training council should meet quarterly or monthly at an hour preceding church training on Sunday evening or on a weekday. (See chapter 5 for detailed planning suggestions.) The meeting should provide opportunities to: (1) examine training needs of church members; (2) make provisions to meet these needs; (3) implement suggestions which grow out of meetings of the council; (4) deal with any problems relating to member training; and (5) review progress and project immediate plans.

Other planning should include the activities necessary to continue enlistment, maintain records, provide socials, etc.

IMPROVING MEMBER TRAINING

Each person involved in church member training should constantly seek to improve the quality of training that is being provided. Areas for improvement include:

1. *Involvement*

(1) What plans were made and carried out to involve all church members in training?

(2) Which of these plans succeeded? to what degree?

(3) What were the problems which need additional planning?

(4) How many church members have not yet been involved in church member training?

(5) How many participated in only part of training offered?

(6) What problems need to be dealt with in the future?

2. Quality

(1) How would you rate the quality of training which has been done during the last quarter and/or year?

(2) What was the general reaction of the people to your approach to church member training?

(3) To what extent have previously made plans improved the quality of training?

3. Evaluating the Success in Achieving Church Goals

The following questions suggest the type of evaluation which can be done:

(1) Was training provided, as needed, for the achievement of church goals? Did some goals receive attention to the exclusion of others? Did other goals receive insufficient attention?

(2) What proportion of church members received training designed to achieve church goals?

(3) What training areas will require additional attention in future planning, especially in regard to continuing or long-range goals?

(4) Was adequate planning for the training done by all officers? What evidence do we have that thorough planning was done? Which areas suffered from the lack of planning? What can be done to correct this in future planning?

(5) What was done to improve the abilities of the training leaders? To what extent were leaders involved in leadership improvement training?

Regular evaluation should be done week by week in each training group. This may be done by the training group leader and the study leader. Monthly or quarterly evaluation should be made by the department directors and the director of church member training. The results of evaluation obviously should lead to plans for improvement.

REACHING CHURCH MEMBERS FOR TRAINING

The enlistment of all of its members in the training ministry is a primary concern of every church. It sets up church training for that purpose. It elects leaders and charges them with the responsibility of reaching all church members for training. The church training director and all of the leadership work at this task.

A church, through its leadership, must assume full responsibility for the development of a church attitude which will make the enlistment of the members easier. What can the pastor and the church leadership do?

1. Develop a Church Conviction That Training Is Imperative

A real church conviction that training the members is imperative is the rich soil out of which grows a great training program. Deep conviction precedes dynamic action in the field of training. It is too much to expect a church to work at something concerning which it has no conviction. The pastor, primarily, is responsible for leading the church to have the conviction that training is imperative. Needless to say, he must have the conviction himself before he can lead the church to have it. In addition to the pastor, all the church training leadership must have this conviction.

The church members who have a conviction that training is imperative are the ones who are most likely to participate in Training Union.

2. Provide Good Leadership

By good leadership is meant the best leadership the church can afford. A church is expected to do the best it can with what it has to offer.

The church training director should be a person of strong influence in the church. A good director of enlistment in church training is also essential for reaching and holding people.

If church training is weak in its leadership, the church is to blame. It is the responsibility of the church to provide good leadership.

3. Provide for Training in the Church Building

In many Baptist churches the training program is restricted severely because of a lack of provision for training in the educational part of the church building.

Every department and training group must have adequate space and equipment to meet their needs. (See age-division books for specific information.)

The proper provision for training in the church building will go a long way toward convincing the people that they ought to be in Training Union.

4. Set Up Sufficient Departments to Make Places for the People

The plan of organization for the training program is so flexible that the church which needs only one unit for each age group can follow the plan without difficulty. Likewise, the larger church which needs multiple departments can have just as many departments as it needs. Within one department just as many training groups as are needed can be set up.

Every church should set up just as many departments and training groups as are needed for training all of the church members. All of the departments needed in the Children and Preschool age groups should be established.

5. Conduct Training Activities Which Attract and Hold People

A church which expects its people to attend church training must develop a program which is worth attending. It must provide good training in the departments and training groups. It must cultivate good Christian fellowship in all of its meetings. To succeed, it must make a vital spiritual contribution to those who are present. This is the task of the leadership.

6. Cooperate with Other Church Programs and Services

Church training does not exist just for itself. It should be church-centered and loyal to the total church program.

Through the church council, the training program can be coordinated properly with all the other church activities so that all may cooperate in the total church program.

7. Promote a Continuous Program of Enlistment

The director of church member training must support the director of enlistment and the enlistment leaders in the training groups in promoting a continuous program of enlistment. Here are suggested steps for such a program:

(1) MAKE A SURVEY OF POSSIBILITIES. The total possibilities for the membership of the church training program may be defined as all the people whose names are on the church roll, all of the children in the families of the church members, and all of the Baptists in the community whose membership is elsewhere, too far away to attend the services of their churches.

The director of enlistment, associate department directors, and enlistment leaders in training groups should study the church roll, the Sunday School roll, and the religious census if the church has had one recently, as the principal sources of information for the possibilities for training.

If necessary, a new survey should be made each year. In most cases it will be necessary to do this.

(2) KEEP THE CHURCH TRAINING ROLL AND PROSPECT LISTS UP TO DATE. Every church training organization should keep a roll of its total membership. Forms for this purpose are available in the Baptist Book Store. This roll should be kept up to date. This, of course, is the responsibility of the secretaries. The information which the roll contains is of inestimable value in enlistment efforts.

From the survey of total possibilities, the prospect lists for all the departments and training groups should be made up. These prospect lists must be kept up to date and new names added as they are available. The director of enlistment should see that all departments have their prospect lists available at all times.

(3) ASSIGN PROSPECTS REGULARLY. The director of enlistment should emphasize enlistment each month. This may be done at the monthly church training council or at some other convenient time.

At the monthly meeting of the church training council the director of enlistment should check carefully with the associate department directors and enlistment leaders of the training groups concerning their prospect lists. New lists should be assigned and, in many cases, names on the old lists reassigned to different groups. Whatever needs to be done should be done regularly so that each worker will have an up-to-date list each month.

(4) VISIT CONTINUOUSLY. In many churches a special day is set aside each week for visitation. Visiting is done during the day and in the evening. All adult and youth members of church training should participate in this visitation. The director of enlistment should make the assignments.

Nothing takes the place of visitation in the building of church training in a church. No church training program will grow without visitation.

(5) GIVE SPECIAL ATTENTION TO NEW MEMBERS. A vital part of the enlistment program of church training is seen in the attention given to new members. These new members should be assimilated into the fellowship of the training groups as quickly as possible.

(6) BE FRIENDLY TO VISITORS. A visitor's card should be filled out by each visitor. He should be introduced to the group. If the training group helps a visitor enjoy and benefit from the meeting, he is likely to come again.

8. Keep the People Coming

(1) ENLIST ALL THE MEMBERS IN ALL THE ACTIVITIES. Members usually become deeply interested in the training program in proportion as they are given opportunity to participate and

contribute to the group. Every member should be enlisted in regular attendance and in all of the activities.

(2) CULTIVATE A VITAL CHRISTIAN FELLOWSHIP. Every meeting is an opportunity for Christian fellowship. It is a good thing for the members of a church to be together often. A church of Christ is in reality a glorious spiritual fellowship of worship, of Bible study, of Christian witnessing, of Christian training, of mutual helpfulness, and a vital Christian service to all mankind. It is the greatest fellowship on earth.

(3) VISIT ABSENTEES REGULARLY. The secretary of each training group should provide a list of absentees at each meeting. This list should be given to the enlistment leader.

The director enlistment should lead all associate department directors and enlistment leaders of the training groups in studying the causes of absenteeism. Is there a lack of personal concern and fellowship? Are the members clannish and inattentive to new members? Perhaps personal work with the officers of the departments and training groups by the director of church training, director of member training, and director of enlistment can solve the problems.

For an effective enlistment program, special emphasis should be given to the following general items:

- Make a survey of the entire church membership to determine prospects. The survey should show correct names, addresses, and telephone numbers.
- Conduct a survey of the training interests of those members who are not now in the training program.
- Plan training projects in keeping with the interests of these unenlisted members.
- Conduct a visitation enlistment program.
- Arrange for announcements to be made from the pulpit.
- Publicize the training opportunities in all church publications.
- Arrange for announcements to be made in Sunday School (departments and classes).
- Feature testimonies by members who are having profitable and enjoyable experiences in training.

- Acquaint the church with progress that is being made in church member training.
- Remember to commend units and leadership when numerical growth takes place.

Remember that the interests of your church members are many and varied. This knowledge should guide you in the choice of periodicals to be used in your regular ongoing church member training. This information should also provide guidance in planning special short-term training projects. Maximum flexibility should be maintained.

SUMMARY

1. Church member training may be described as training to equip members to participate in the life and work of the church in the world.
2. The organization a church has should provide the best way to move toward implementing the tasks of church member training.
3. Each church should analyze its training needs and determine the amount and type of organization required.
4. When a church does not have a director of church member training, the functions should be performed by the church training director.
5. Two types of member training need to be planned:
   (1) that which is done on a continuing basis
   (2) that which is done on a short-term basis
6. Each person involved in church member training should constantly seek to improve the quality of training which is being provided.

Chapter Nine

LEADER TRAINING

EVERY CHURCH needs dedicated trained leaders with ability and determination to achieve their purposes in service. Vacant places of leadership in a church point to a need for an organized effort to discover and develop members for service. A failing outreach, an ineffective witness, and a shriveling ministry give evidence of a church's neglect in developing members for service. The fault can be a church's reliance upon a few members to do the work of many.

QUEST FOR AN EFFECTIVE CHURCH

In most churches, leaders need to be relieved of some of their responsibilities so that they may function more effectively. Most leaders are in need of continuing training to develop and increase their ability to serve. Their present leadership responsibilities may allow neither the time nor the energy for improvement. Many leaders are suffering from leadership fatigue.

Programs are only what leaders make them. Leaders aren't born —they are "born again" in Jesus Christ and have the opportunity of growing through faith and determination. The dynamic faith of a growing child of God can lead him to "pay the price" necessary to become a more effective worker.

Many of today's adult church members are "spectators waiting to be entertained." They are apathetic, spiritual infants possessing the characteristics of an infant-like mind in a mature body. The tragedy of the spiritual neglect of one or more generations of Southern Baptists has provided an increasing weight of leadership responsibility which must hang around the necks of a few dedicated workers.

Reclaiming these products of neglect and redirecting them toward paths of useful service can be one of the greater services of church leader training. The discovery of persons with the potential to lead requires a unique insight into the dormant spirits of inactive church members. The enlistment of leaders is more than guiding obviously interested persons into a course of study.

Recruiting activities range from the guiding of the eager to the stirring of the indifferent. A church cannot afford to overlook its responsibility to each person. Encouraging, fanning the spark, pleading, and praying are all part of the enlistment effort. Faith in people, faith in God's ability to make people feel useful, and the patience and forbearance to nudge them along become worthy characteristics of those who would enlist leaders.

ORGANIZING LEADER TRAINING

People must make things happen. Leader training has been neglected because churches lack confidence in their ability to provide this level of training. Churches can begin a specific approach to leader development by providing the basic organization, a department, or a unit of leader training. Elect a director of church leader training. Instruct him to determine the leadership potential and the leadership needs of the church. Armed with this knowledge, he can recommend the amount of organization required to carry out his assignment. The following patterns of organization may suggest ways of meeting the needs that have been discovered.

One way to organize for leader training is for the director to serve as instructor for a short-term course which meets at the same time as member training activities. A church with only one unit of organization for each age division may choose to use this method to organize its leader training.

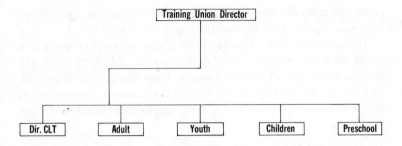

A slight change in organization would allow one or more persons to assist with the instruction by either serving as assistants or by teaching specific units within a course. For example, the pastor could assist by teaching a unit on the Bible or Baptist doctrine which may be part of an introductory course for potential leaders.

The more developed the leadership training requirements be-

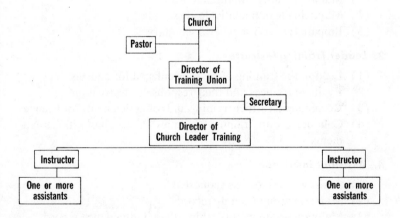

come, the more the organization will require expansion. The following chart suggests how the functions may be divided.

The following duties identify work which needs to be done in a leader training program. As a church is able to add additional workers, the duties of each worker becomes more specialized. When one or two persons are responsible for the entire leader training effort, they are required to assume the essential duties of several of these positions.

1. *Director of Church Leader Training*

The director of leader training is responsible to the director of church training for planning, conducting, and evaluating the leader training program for the church. He is responsible for coordinating special leader training projects.

The duties of the director of church leader training are given in detail in chapter 3.

2. *Secretary-Leader Training*

    (1) Maintain leader training records
    (2) Maintain file of potential leaders
    (3) Prepare reports for general secretary

3. *Leader Training Instructor*

    (1) Lead in the training of persons enlisted for courses
    (2) Evaluate trainees and their response to instruction
    (3) Recommend further training and/or assignments for trainees
    (4) Conduct group training activities in keeping with assignments

4. *Assistant Instructor*

    (1) Assist with courses as requested
    (2) Maintain group training records
    (3) Maintain group membership roll and attendance record

RESOURCES FOR LEADER TRAINING

Special materials are available for courses of study. However, "resources" for leader training include a number of items. Space, time, equipment, materials, supplies, funds, relationships within the church, and even community training resources should be considered in developing an adequate training program. Each of these items will be considered briefly in this chapter. A more comprehensive treatment appears in the *Church Leader Training Handbook*.

1. Space

The same space available for other adult training groups should be adequate as a beginning. However, space may need to be assigned exclusively to the leader training department. Leader training activities may never involve large numbers. Groups may meet at many different times of the week. Some displays and exhibits may need to remain in place for several training sessions. Ideally, a classroom suitable for the use of audiovisual materials is desirable.

2. Time

Church leaders should not "build fences around programs" by the definite assignment of specific times for meetings. Wherever possible, church leaders should allow the leader training department to work out its own schedule so as to provide courses at times most suitable for trainees.

3. Equipment

Perhaps some of the equipment needed for leader training will already be in department or classrooms and can be used by other programs of the church.

Some furnishings and equipment needed for leader training may not be appropriate for use in regular educational activities of a church. (Teaching machines, viewers for individual use, headsets, and other special materials sometimes available for leader training may not be practical for use in other departments.) Churches may be tempted to secure only those items which can be used for other church activities. However, a well-equipped leader training department may produce more workers who are better equipped to do their jobs.

The criteria for selecting furnishings and equipment should be the value of the item for training purposes, the amount of use it will get, and the availability of qualified users.

Trainees should understand the intended use of equipment and become proficient in the use of all items available for instructional purposes. Instructors should develop training plans which utilize available equipment to help the trainee learn the subject under study and to help him become acquainted with good techniques in using the furnishings and equipment.

The following equipment is suggested in order of preference. Items in the left column are basic:

easels	overhead projectors
chalkboards	mimeograph equipment
tack boards	copy machines (church office)
record players	photographic equipment
tape recorders	video-tape equipment
projectors (slide,	teaching machines
filmstrips,	
motion picture)	

The size of the church, the extent of its training program, financial resources, and availability of workers qualified to use the equipment, will determine how much equipment a church should supply. Equipment should be selected according to degree of need and practical usage in training activities.

4. Materials and Supplies

Trainees and leaders will need study materials in the form of textbooks, workbooks, church literature, supplementary curriculum pieces, promotional literature, and general supplies.

A church should decide to supply these items as needed to all trainees and leaders. In some cases, these may be textbooks loaned by the church library. In other situations, each trainee may be given personal copies which can be marked and used later as reference material.

Every trainee should be given current copies of the general program magazines, age-division materials appropriate to his personal use, and all materials related to the specific position for which he or she is preparing.

There are many items of promotional literature which relate to the training of workers. These can be assembled as part of a notebook or made available to the trainee who will be encouraged to build his own set of reference materials.

Materials intended for use in training sessions as "handouts" should be of a standard format, so as to be easily included in a standard reference file or notebook. A department may desire to give notebooks, file folders, or accordian files to trainees to encourage the development of a reference library for his particular job.

The indexed accordian-type file is an ideal aid. Textbooks, promotional items, mimeographed materials, etc., can be classified by topic and placed in assigned file pockets. The file can be easily carried and will aid the trainee in keeping materials together.

The instructor will need access to mimeograph supplies, poster materials, literature, office supplies, letterheads, postage, and a variety of special materials. Since these are items used in regular church activities, they may be secured from the church office as needed or stored in limited quantities in the leader training department. Such things as poster board, marking pens, and masking tape may also be stored in the department.

The church library should be a source of materials for leader training. In addition to the required textbooks, trainees should have access to a large number of books that will help them in specific areas and provide broad background material for leadership. Some of the texts will be in content areas. Guided reading plans should be developed by the instructor in cooperation with the church library staff. Trainees should be encouraged to read and report as a part of their instruction.

PLANNING AND CONDUCTING LEADER TRAINING

Earlier in this chapter, emphasis was placed upon determining needs and resources before establishing the organization. However, after the organization has been established, decisions will need to be made concerning what is to be done, by whom, when, and to whom.

Determining the answers to these and other questions which may arise is a way of planning. Planning requires knowing where we are going; knowing where we are going suggests having goals.

Goals, both short-range and long-range, must be established if church members are to be trained to meet tomorrow's (short-range) and the day-after-tomorrow's (long-range) needs. If training is left to chance without adequate planning, many church members will continue to find that they are not qualified to do the jobs of tomorrow. What are the training goals of a church? How will the mission and function of the church of tomorrow compare with the needs the church must meet in the world about it? What planned and scheduled training will be needed during the next few years in order to meet the leadership needs of the churches?

Only the church training council will be able to establish the goals which meet the challenge of the church's training program. The training council must develop and put into written form training goals which will meet the needs of a church desiring to provide exceptional service. The director of church leader training must translate these goals into actions which will lead to their achievement.

In churches not having a director of church leader training, the church training director will be responsible for detailed planning of the leader training activities. In some cases, it may be more practical to ask an Adult department director to coordinate leader training projects along with the member training projects in his department. The department director will then plan with the person selected to lead the project.

In preparing to conduct training projects, the leaders should be particularly careful not to disrupt regular activities of the church. Guidelines should be established which will help them to avoid depleting other units of organization of their needed leadership. A set of suggested guidelines follows:

1. Guidelines for Leader Training Groups

(1) The church council makes studies to determine training needs of the church. The pastor, minister of education, and director of church training may direct this study.

(2) The council adopts the schedule for the project.

(3) The director of church leader training, or the director of church training, assigns a suitable meeting place with equipment needed for the project.

(4) Enrolment for the project is open to selected persons enlisted by special invitation.

(5) Present leaders of training groups are not eligible to attend unless they are replaced by qualified leaders. Care is exercised not to deplete a training group of its members.

(6) The director of church leader training, or the director of church training, stands ready to help enlist persons to conduct the project and to secure needed training aids and materials.

(7) Enrolment and attendance record forms are prepared and provided by church training. Appropriate reports are to be submitted to the general secretary of the training program before the close of each session.

(8) Persons enrolled in the projects are encouraged to continue their training by participating in regular training groups provided for their age, or to enrol in another short-term project upon completion of their present course.

2. Guidelines for Members of Training Groups

Some definite understandings are needed concerning the trainees and their other activities during a training course. Leader training projects are more demanding than other educational activities, therefore, trainees must be protected from overloading. The following suggestions may help to prevent trainees from becoming discouraged and desiring to drop out of a course.

Training will be ineffective unless trainees apply themselves faithfully to their learning tasks. The following guidelines are suggested:

(1) All trainees will complete required reading during the course. Study course credit will be given for each book studied upon completion of the course.

(2) All trainees will report five minutes before each session so

that the session can begin on time. (This will also help to establish a good habit for future service.)

(3) Trainees are expected to be present for every session. Anticipated absences should be reported to the leader so that assignments can be made to keep the trainees on schedule. All absences will require makeup work.

(4) Trainees will not accept assignments—such as substitute teachers, leaders of assembly programs, or as participants in any other activity—which will conflict with training sessions.

(5) No grades will be given. However, to graduate from the course, trainees must read the required textbooks and attend every session or complete all makeup work for the sessions missed.

(6) Trainees will also be required to complete regular assignments and participate in one or more evaluation sessions in which their future training plans can be initiated.

IMPROVING LEADER TRAINING

Before a program can be improved, there must be means of evaluating its present status. Leaders should:

1. Know the leader training needs of the church
2. Be able to determine how effectively these needs are being met
3. Report and evaluate periodically

Surveys taken prior to the organization of leader training in the church training program will reveal the needs of the church and the degree to which groups are working together. The first effort at improvement may be in the area of relationships to other programs. Developing a better understanding of program needs and how these can best be met is a worthy objective for any director.

Continual updating of these surveys will indicate the increase or decrease in the number of vacancies. Also, attention to the results in each program will indicate changes in the quality of the work being done.

The training reports will reflect basic statistical information while courses are in progress. Inconsistent patterns of participation, high rates of trainee dropouts, and similar items point to internal group problems. The director of leader training should continually use these tools to know the status of current training and to watch for evidences of problems. Frequent consultation with workers will help to maintain a high level of efficiency.

Leader training may also be improved by securing better equipment and through updating training techniques. Helping instructors to improve their skills and providing them with adequate materials and equipment may be the most efficient way of upgrading a leader training program.

RECRUITING CHURCH MEMBERS FOR LEADER TRAINING

Training is a process. It is more than the acquiring of knowledge. Training includes the acquisition of attitudes, understandings, and skills. The influence of the instructor or trainer may be greater than that of the "content" of the course. Leader training is a contagion. Attitudes and understandings come through association with dedicated leaders, through the trials of the learning experience, through the joy and exhilaration associated with success or accomplishment, and through accomplishing worthy goals.

1. Discover Leadership Potential

Many persons in today's churches need help in discovering and developing their leadership potential. A potential leader is not limited by his past but rather by his lack of vision of his future in Christ. He must learn to "walk in faith," to "run the race," and to "press toward the mark." He must discover the Paulinian faith which said, "I can do all things through Christ." He must be "enabled" by the equipping for service. This is the task of leader training. It requires a church to analyze and determine its leadership needs.

A church may engage in a number of different actions which will help its members strike the chord of their potential as leaders. Talent surveys, manpower studies, and studies of qualifications and special skills possessed by members are a few of the more obvious actions. Helping members to match their professional skills with those required by positions of service in their church is an unequalled opportunity.

A church should be aware of the tremendous leadership potential of its youth. Recognizing Youth's ability to lead and providing opportunities for service through special youth projects are important tools of leadership discovery. Approaches to the discovery of potential leaders should include enlistment of the masses of the inactive into introductory courses in leadership.

2. Involving Members in Preservice Training

Preservice training is for persons who have never held a church-elected place of service, persons who have not recently held a place of service, or persons who are preparing to accept a different type of responsibility. The training includes counseling or self-evaluation tools which will enable the trainee to develop an adequate training plan in keeping with personal goals and church leadership needs. Time permitting, persons could be given extensive training in the categories described under "Content for Leader Training Courses" in this chapter before beginning to serve. However, the need for workers may limit the amount of preservice training to that which qualifies the trainee for the minimum level of performance required for the job.

3. Involving Leaders in In-service Training

In-service training is for all persons currently holding church-elected positions. It assists leaders in determining their training needs and in securing the appropriate training. In-service training is a means of providing additional training to help leaders qualify for or to function more effectively in their present place of service. Most in-service training will be provided as either "on-the-job" training or as a special training group which meets at a time which does not interfere with normal job responsibilities.

Another type of in-service training which should be considered is the "internship." A person may be selected to serve as an associate to an experienced leader so as to learn the job.

CONTENT FOR LEADER TRAINING COURSES

Leader training materials are prepared in a variety of formats. Some are designed for extensive use by training groups. Special materials are available for individual use in home study. Others may be adapted for either individual or group use.

Leader training materials in the New Church Study Course are grouped as follows:

General Leadership Training

1. Introductory Courses in Church Leadership
2. Understanding Work with Age Levels and Special Groups in a Church
3. Developing General Leadership Skills

Specialized Leadership Training

1. Bible Teaching Program
2. Training Program
3. Church Missions Program—Woman's Missionary Union
4. Church Missions Program—Brotherhood
5. Church Music Program
6. Pastoral Ministries
7. Program and Administrative Services

SUMMARY

1. Every church needs dedicated trained leaders with ability and determination to achieve the training goals of the church.
2. Almost all churches need additional leaders.
3. Most leaders need extra training to improve their performances.
4. A church needs to carefully evaluate its leader training needs before beginning a program of leader training.
5. Leader training projects are often more demanding than other educational activities.
6. Leader training materials are available in a variety of formats.
7. The *Church Leader Training Handbook* provides additional guidance for planning and conducting leader training in a church.

Personal Learning Activities

Chapter 1

1. Training may be either _____ or _____.
2. Church training gives attention to three factors related to improved performance. These factors are _____, _____, and _____.
3. Four broad areas are included in the church training curriculum. These are Christian theology, Christian ethics, _____ and church polity and organization.

Chapter 2

4. Organization should be a servant, not a _____.
5. The Training Union organization should be simple and _____.
6. The three types of training offered in church training are: New Church Member Orientation, Church Training, and _____ _____ Training.

Chapter 3

7. Cultivation of a church conviction and a positive attitude toward training depends more upon the _____ than on any other person.
8. The call to discipleship is a call to _____.
9. The development of leaders begins with evaluation of their abilities and _____.
10. Leader training courses may be taken as preservice or _____-_____ training.

Chapter 4

11. The _____ _____ is the most valuable resource in Christian education.
12. The church training periodical for general officers is the _____ _____ magazine.
13. The New Church Study Course includes the Christian Development Courses and the _____ _____ Courses.

116

Chapter 5

14. Planning gives leaders a sense of _____ and
_____.

15. The director of church training may plan on a cycle basis or on a
_____ _____ basis.

16. The church council and the _____ council are the
chief planning bodies of the church training program.

Chapter 6

17. There are two types of evaluation needed in a church training program, process evaluation and _____ evaluation.

18. The _____ _____ has the primary responsibility for evaluating the church's training program.

19. The key to evaluation is _____ and the key to
_____ is evaluation.

Chapter 7

20. In a small church, new member orientation may be carried on by
_____ persons(s).

21. _____ different pieces of curriculum materials are available for new member orientation classes.

22. Financial resources for new member orientation should be provided
through the _____ _____.

Chapter 8

23. The primary constituency of church training is _____
_____ and their _____.

24. The two types of church member training are those done on a continuing basis and those done on a _____-_____
basis.

25. Regular _____ should be done week by week in each
training group.

Chapter 9

26. Every church needs _____ _____ _____ with ability and
determination to achieve their purposes in service.

27. Additional guidance for the director of church leader training may
be found in the _____ _____ _____
_____.

28. The New _____ _____ _____
contains material to use in leadership training.

The New Church Study Course

THE NEW CHURCH STUDY COURSE effective in January 1970, is based on more than three years of study and design. It offers several improvements in the Church Study Course, which began in October 1959. At that time, three courses previously promoted by the Sunday School Board were merged: the Sunday School Training Course, the Graded Training Union Study Course, and the Church Music Training Course. Principles and methods books of the Woman's Missionary Union and the Brotherhood Commission were added in October 1961 and January 1967 respectively.

The New Church Study Course offers increased flexibility in meeting the needs of Southern Baptists. It provides courses of varying length and difficulty, varied formats and types of course materials, additional types of credit, and improved organization of courses.

The New Church Study Course consists of two types of courses: Christian Development Courses for all church members, and Christian Leadership Courses for church leaders. Courses are organized into subject areas.

The purpose of the Christian Development Courses is to provide study which will help church members grow toward maturity in Christian living and competence in Christian service. These courses offer more comprehensive, advanced, and varied learning experiences in subject areas of a church's educational program than can be provided through curriculum periodicals. Tests and exercises, credits, and diplomas of achievement which help church members measure their progress in developing needed knowledge, understanding, and skills are included in some courses. Units of instruction are provided for Preschoolers and Children. These are designed to reinforce foundational learnings. Materials which churches may use in recognizing the participation of Children in these units are available from Baptist Book Stores.

The Christian Leadership Courses provide a comprehensive series of courses organized into subject areas dealing with knowledge, understandings, and skills needed for effective church leadership. Tests and exercises, credits, and diplomas to help leaders measure their growth in

118

leadership ability are included in some courses. The Christian Leadership Courses are the primary source for leadership training materials prepared by the agencies cooperating in the New Church Study Course.

Courses of both types are designed to be effective for individual and class study. Learning aids, study guides, and teaching guides are available for some courses. Credits are granted to Youth and Adults for reading, individual study, and class study.

The New Church Study Course is promoted by the Baptist Sunday School Board, 127 Ninth Avenue, North, Nashville, Tennessee 37203, through the departments in the Education Division; by the Woman's Missionary Union, 600 North Twentieth Street, Birmingham, Alabama 35203; by the Brotherhood Commission, 1548 Poplar Avenue, Memphis, Tennessee 38104; and by the respective departments in the state conventions affiliated with the Southern Baptist Convention.

A record of all credits and diplomas earned should be maintained in each church.

Detailed information about the course, the system of credits and diplomas, and the keeping of records is available from the agencies listed above.

Forms for keeping records may be ordered from any Baptist Book Store.

Requirements for Credit

THIS BOOK is the text for course 6402 of the Training Program subject area in the Christian Leadership Courses of the New Church Study Course. If credit is desired for this course through class study, individual study, or reading, the following requirements must be met:

CLASSWORK

1. This course is designed for seven and one half (7½) hours of class study and carries three (3) credits for such usage. If the course is studied in a class setting of less than seven and one half (7½) hours, the following criteria apply:
   (1) Five (5) class hours—two (2) credits
   (2) Two and one half class hours—one (1) credit
   The teacher will indicate the length of the class and the number of credits to be granted on Form 151, Request for Course Credit (revised).

   For courses in which laboratory experience or practice is desirable, two hours of such guided experience may be substituted as one (1) hour of class time, provided at least half of the required hours are actually spent in classwork.
2. A class member who attends all class sessions and completes the reading of the book as directed by the teacher will not be required to do any written work for credit.
3. A class member who is absent from one or more sessions must complete the required exercises or questions in the "Personal Learning Activities" section on all chapters he misses. In such a case, he must turn in his paper by the date the teacher sets (usually within ten days following the last class). Also, he must certify that he has read the book.
4. The teacher should request credits for himself. A person who teaches a course for Youth or Adults (in any subject area) will be granted the same number of credits as class members. The teacher of an approved unit of study of Preschoolers and Children will be granted two credits in course 6199 of Understanding Work with Age Levels

and Special Groups in a Church subject area in the Christian Leadership Courses. Request credits on Form 151.

5. The church training director, or the person designated by the church, should complete Form 151, Request for Course Credit (revised), and forward it after completion of the class to the Church Study Course Awards Office, 127 Ninth Avenue, North, Nashville, Tennessee 37203.

INDIVIDUAL STUDY

1. A person who wishes to complete this course without attending class sessions may receive full credit by certifying that he has read the book and has completed all exercises or questions in the "Personal Learning Activities" section.
2. Students may find profit in studying the text together, but individual papers are required. Carbon copies or duplicates of the answers cannot be accepted.
3. The work required for individual study credit should be turned in for checking to the church training director or to the person designated by the church to administer the New Church Study Course. Form 151, Request for Course Credit (revised), must be used in requesting credit. It is to be forwarded by the church training director, or the person designated by the church, to the Church Study Course Awards Office, 127 Ninth Avenue, North, Nashville, Tennessee 37203.

READING CREDIT

1. A person may receive one credit toward the diploma on which he is working by reading this book.
2. Upon completion of the reading, he must complete Form 151, Request for Course Study (revised). He should give the completed form to the church training director or to the person designated by his church to be responsible for administering the New Church Study Course.
3. The church training director or the person designated by the church will see that the request is completed, signed, and forwarded to the Church Study Course Awards Office, 127 Ninth Avenue, North, Nashville, Tennessee 37203.

AWARDS AND RECORDS

Two copies of the course credit award form will be sent by the Study Course Awards Office to the church. The original copy should be filed in the church training and the duplicate given to the individual.

Church Training Achievement Guide

(Effective Oct. 1, 1970)

Purpose

THE CHURCH TRAINING ACHIEVEMENT GUIDE is designed to help a church plan, conduct, improve, and evaluate its training program. The pastor and church training director should lead the church training council to use this guide in accomplishing the church's training tasks.

Nine areas are included in the guide. These are: Program Foundations, Program, Relationships, Organization, Leaders and Members, Physical Resources, Finances, Planning and Evaluation, and Records and Reports. For each of these areas, there is a statement of purpose and a list of achievements.

Levels of Achievement

There are three levels of achievement. These are: *Merit, Advanced,* and *Distinguished.* These are reached in the following manner:

A church is eligible for Merit recognition:
    (1) When its training program completes twenty achievements in the Merit column;
    (2) When all achievements marked with an asterisk (*) are included; and
    (3) When at least one age division has received recognition for Merit achievement.

A church is eligible for Advanced recognition:
    (1) When its training program completes twenty achievements in the Merit column as noted above;
    (2) When it also completes fifteen achievements in the Advanced column, including those marked with an asterisk (*); and
    (3) When at least two age divisions have received recognition for Merit achievement.

A church is eligible for Distinguished recognition when:
    (1) Its training program completes twenty-five achievements in the

Merit column and twenty-five achievements in the Advanced column;

(2) When all achievements marked with asterisks (*) are included; and

(3) When at least one age division has received recognition for Advanced achievement.

Each paragraph of the guide, whether in the Merit column or the Advanced column, constitutes an achievement. Certain achievements are stated to show an achievement already completed during the church year. Other achievements are stated in the present tense to suggest the continuation of an achievement up to the time application for recognition is made. Example: "Church training leaders plan efforts to discover potential leaders not now participating in training."

Where appropriate, an achievement in the Advanced column may grow out of an achievement in the Merit column to represent a higher level of work in the same area. Example: Achievements 3a and 3b in the Advanced column grow out of achievement 3 in the Merit column.

At many points in the Guide, the completion of an achievement in the Advanced column also presupposes the completion of the corresponding achievement in the Merit column. Example: Achievements 4a and 4. When 4a is achieved, 4 can also be checked as completed.

Paragraphs are spaced to show this relationship.

Definition of Terms Used

TYPE OF TRAINING—Three types of training are included in the training program of a church. These are: new church member orientation, church member training, and church leader training. Each type of training is related to a specific target group in the church's membership, as noted in the designation for each.

ONGOING CHURCH MEMBER TRAINING—The regular week-by-week training usually done in age-division departments and training groups on Sunday evening. However, it may be scheduled at times other than Sunday evening.

SHORT-TERM TRAINING PROJECT—A training activity which has a definite beginning and ending time. It involves a specific group of people and seeks to accomplish a specific purpose which is not being achieved by the ongoing church training program.

While the ongoing program of church training is designed for *all* church members and provides comprehensiveness, continuity, sequence and balance, short-term training is provided for short periods to selected groups. Such groups are determined by the purpose to be accomplished. Examples: Training sessions for parents (not enrolled in ongoing program) of teen-agers, or, a study course on doctrine for a group of adults not enrolled in ongoing training program.

TRAINING GROUP—Any group organized to provide training, either ongoing or short-term. Examples include: departments, classes for new member orientation, classes for church leaders, training groups within departments, etc.

CHURCH TRAINING COUNCIL—The group of leaders responsible for planning, conducting, and evaluating the church's training program. The church training director serves as chairman of the council. The pastor, other staff members and other general officers, including directors of types of training, and age-division directors, make up the council. The church which has only departments and training groups in church member training may include department and training group leaders; in the council.

Applying for Recognition

A church may apply for recognition at any time. Recognition will be granted at any time during the church year (October–September) for that particular year. Church leaders will determine when sufficient achievements have been completed for a particular level of achievement and will complete application for appropriate recognition.

A church may apply for more than one level of recognition within a church year, at different times during the year. Also, recognition on more than one level of achievement may be applied for at the same time. Such achievement should be indicated on the completed application blank.

All requests for recognition should be submitted to the state convention Church Training Department serving your state.

I. PROGRAM FOUNDATIONS

Achievements in this section guide church training leaders in understanding the biblical teachings, concepts, objectives, and needs which serve as the foundations of the church training program.

Merit Achievement	Advanced Achievement
*1. Each member of the Church training council has earned New Church Study Course credit for reading *A Dynamic Church.*	*1a. Fifty percent of the members of the church training council have received New Church Study Course credit for individual or class study of *A Dynamic Church.*

II. PROGRAM

Church training leaders need to understand and use effectively the activities and approaches suggested in this section to help them accomplish their training tasks.

Merit Achievement	Advanced Achievement
*2. Church training provides graded weekly training opportunities for church members and their families.	*2a. Church training leaders conducted during the year at least one short-term training project designed to train persons to worship, witness, learn, minister, or apply.
	2b. At least one Adult training group studied during the year an approved unit with members earning New Church Study Course awards in the Lesson Course Study Plan.[1]
*3. The church training program provides orientation for new church members.	*3a. The church training program provides counseling and instruction for new church members with 60 percent of them completing orientation during the year.
4. Church training leaders plan efforts to enlist new church members in other training groups appropriate to their needs upon their completion of orientation sessions.	4a. Church training leaders enlisted one half of the new church members who completed orientation during the year in other appropriate training groups.

---

1. A plan through which Adults may earn awards in the New Church Study Course for study of an approved curriculum unit in their respective training groups. For further details, see Adult leadership periodicals.

II. PROGRAM—Continued

5. Church training leaders plan efforts to discover potential leaders not now participating in training.

5a. Church training leaders conducted during the year a Christian Service Survey to discover potential leaders not now participating in training.

6a. Church training leaders maintain a current file of potential leaders for the church.

*6. The church training program provides training opportunities for leaders and potential leaders, in addition to the training received in member training groups.

*6b. The church training program provides a course of instruction for potential leaders for the church.

6c. The church training program provides training for leaders now in service, and offers training as needed for all church programs.

7. Church training leaders conducted during the year at least one special project, such as Youth Week, Church Member Training Week, or Christian Home Week.

7a. The church training program provided during the year short-term training in support of at least one special project of the church.

8. The church training program gave special emphasis during the year in support of at least two denominational causes, such as Cooperative Program, Week of Prayer for Foreign Missions, etc.

9. The church training program provides vocational guidance for its leaders and members.

II. PROGRAM—Continued

10. The church training program provides guidance in family living for its leaders and members.

III. RELATIONSHIPS

Achievements in this section guide church training leaders in maintaining essential associations with persons or groups for the purposes of coordination.

Merit Achievement	Advanced Achievement
*11. The director of church training consults with the pastor, church staff, and leaders of other church organizations in planning the training program.	*11a. The director of church training, as a member of the church council, helps plan, coordinate, and evaluate the total church program.
12. Church training leaders participated during the year in at least one associational activity related to church training.	12a. Church training leaders participated during the year in two or more associational activities related to their area of work in the church training program.
	12b. Church training leaders participated in at least one state or Southern Baptist Convention activity related to church training.
13. Church training leaders promoted the training clinic[2] conducted by associational Training Union.	13a. Church training leaders worked with church general officers and committees to provide at least one training opportunity during the year.

2. An associational clinic sponsored by Training Union and designed to train church council members, church general officers, and committee members.

IV. ORGANIZATION

Achievements in this section help church training leaders identify training jobs to be done, group them accordingly, and assign persons to do them.

Merit Achievement	Advanced Achievement
14. The church training program provides organization for graded ongoing training opportunities designed to meet church and individual training needs.	14a. The church training program provided during the year organization for two or more short-term training opportunities in church member training.
*15. The church training council is composed of the church training director, general secretary, and a representative from each age division included in the church's training program.	*15a. The church training council is composed of the church training director, director of enlistment, general secretary, and the director of each type of training included in the training program, and the director of each age division.
16. The church training program provides organization for the orientation of new church members.	16a. The church training program provides organization for the orientation of new church members through graded counseling and instruction.
17. The church training program provides organization for at least one of the following: (1) General leader training (2) Specialized leader training	17a. The church training program provides organization for a course of instruction for potential leaders. 17b. The church training program provides organization for two or more short-term training opportunities in church leader training.
18. Each church-elected training leader is provided a statement of duties pertaining to his office.	

V. LEADERS AND MEMBERS

Achievements in this section help a church enlist and train the leaders and members necessary to carry out its various training activities.

Merit Achievement	Advanced Achievement
19. The church elected all church training leaders according to the church plan.	
20. The church training program has the following leaders: director, associate director, general secretary, and at least one leader for each department and training group.	20a. The church training program has the following leaders: director, general secretary, director of enlistment, a director for at least one type of training, and one or more leaders for each age division in church member training.
	20b. The church training program has the following leaders: director, director of enlistment, directors for two or more types of training, general secretary, and two or more leaders for each age division in church member training.
21. Church training leaders interpreted training opportunities in congregational services and/or church organizational meetings at least once each quarter.	21a. Church training leaders made two or more special efforts to enlist new members on the basis of interest in, and need for, a particular curriculum study.
22. Church training leaders maintain an up-to-date prospect file for use in enlisting persons for training.	22a. Church training leaders assign names of prospects for visitation on a regular plan.

V. LEADERS AND MEMBERS—Continued

23. Church training leaders conduct at least one visitation effort each quarter to enlist persons in training.

23a. Church training leaders conduct one visitation effort each month to enlist persons in training.

24. The number enrolled in the ongoing member training program equals one third of the resident church membership.

24a. The total number enrolled in the church training program (all types of training) equals one half of the resident church members.

*25. Each member of the church training council has earned New Church Study Course credit for reading ADMINISTERING CHURCH TRAINING.

*25a. Seventy-five percent of the members of the church training council have earned New Church Study Course credit for individual or class study of ADMINISTERING CHURCH TRAINING.

*26. All of the church-elected church training leaders have received a New Church Study Course credit for reading the age division manuals related to their work.

*26a. Fifty percent of the church-elected church training leaders have earned New Church Study Course credit for individual or class study of the age division manuals related to their work.

27. Twenty-five percent of the church elected church training leaders have earned New Church Study Course credit for reading the *guiding* and the *understanding* books related to the age division with which they work.

27a. Fifty percent of the church elected church training leaders have earned New Church Study Course credit for individual or class study of the *guiding* and the *understanding* books related to the age division with which they work.

V. LEADERS AND MEMBERS—Continued

28. The church training program has provided at least one annual opportunity for all church members to earn credit in the New Church Study Course.

28a. Each member of the church training council has earned credit in the New Church Study Course for study of books in the Christian Leadership Course.

28b. The church training program has provided during the year two or more opportunities for all church members to earn credit in the New Church Study Course.

VI. PHYSICAL RESOURCES

Achievements in this section help church training leaders request and use the space, equipment, supplies, and furnishings supplied by the church for carrying on its training program.

Merit Achievement	Advanced Achievement
29. Church training leaders assign and use the physical resources provided by the church.	29a. Needs for special kinds of space, equipment, or supplies for various types of training have been reported through appropriate channels.
30. Church training leaders determined the physical resources needed during the year for the church's training program and reported findings to the church.	30a. Church training leaders determined additional physical resources to be needed by the training program during a three year period and reported these anticipated needs to the church.
*31. *Church Training,* the general leadership periodical, is provided for all church training general officers.	

VI. PHYSICAL RESOURCES—Continued

*32. Southern Baptist Convention graded curriculum materials are provided for church training leaders and members.

32a. Supplementary materials (curriculum supplements, books, pamphlets, etc.) are provided, as requested, for church training leaders and members.

33. Church training leaders recommended the establishment or improvement of a church library.

33a. Church training leaders work with Church Library leaders in securing supplementary materials, such as films, filmstrips, New Church Study Course books, recordings, and other resources, and encourage leaders and members to use these materials in conducting various training sessions.

VII. FINANCES

Achievements in this section help leaders request and use the money which a church provides to carry on its training program.

Merit Achievement	Advanced Achievement
*34. Church training leaders determined and requested the budget needed during the year for conducting the training program.	34a. Church training leaders determined long-range (three to five years) budget needs and reported these needs through appropriate channels.

VIII. PLANNING AND EVALUATIONS

Achievements in this section help church training leaders determine in detail what will be done for a specific period of time, and provide opportunities at appropriate intervals to measure the effectiveness of the work which has been completed.

Merit Achievement	Advanced Achievement
*35. Church training leaders met during the year to plan and evaluate the church's training program.	35a. The church training council developed a written plan of training activities for the current year.
	35b. The church training council met at least four times during the year to plan, coordinate, and evaluate the church's training program.
	35c. The church training council met at least once each month to plan, coordinate, and evaluate the church's training program.
36. The general leadership periodical, *Church Training* is used in planning the church's training program.	
37. Church training leaders annually determine and schedule training opportunities which relate to the total church program.	37a. Church training leaders develop an annual calendar of training activities to be included in the church calendar.

IX. RECORDS AND REPORTS

Achievements in this section help church training leaders obtain appropriate information about the church's training program and share it with the church and the denomination.

IX. RECORDS AND REPORTS—Continued

Merit Achievement	Advanced Achievement
38. The church training program uses Southern Baptist records and report forms.	
*39. The church training director reports regularly to the church according to the church plan.	*39a. The church training director submits to the church a written, monthly report of enrolment, attendance, and activities.
40. The church training director reports annually to the church.	
41. The church training director reports annually to the state convention Church Training Department the names and addresses of church-elected church training leaders.	
42. Church training leaders use records and reports to evaluate the church training program.	

Recognition Request

CHURCH TRAINING ACHIEVEMENT GUIDE

THIS FORM should be filled out and sent to your state convention Church Training department. The state convention secretary will verify the request and forward it to the Church Training Department, Baptist Sunday School Board, which will send the certificates for achievement.

We request: (check one)　　　　　　　　Date _____ 19___

We have completed the achievements which are circled below. Asterisks (*) indicate required items.

RECOGNITION REQUEST—Continued

Merit Recognition ☐   Advanced Recognition ☐
Distinguished Recognition ☐

We have achieved Merit recognition in the following age divisions:
(check appropriate blanks)
Adult ___ Youth ___ Children ___
Preschool ___

We have achieved Advanced recognition in the following age divisions:
(check appropriate blanks)
Adult ___ Youth ___ Children ___
Preschool ___

Merit				Advanced			
*1	*11	21	*31	*1a	*11a	21a	
*2	12	22	*32	*2a	12a	22a	32a
*3	13	23	33	2b	12b	23a	33a
4	14	24	34	*3a	13a	24a	
5	*15	*25	*35	4a	14a	*25a	34a
*6	16	*26	36		*15a		
7	17	27	37	5a	16a	*26a	35a
8	18	28	38	6a	17a	27a	35b
9	19	29	*39	*6b	17b	27b	35c
10	20	30	40			28a	
			41			28b	
			42	6c	20a	29a	37a
				7a	20b	30a	38a
							*39a

Please send recognition
certificate to:

_____
(Name)

_____
(Church)

_____
(Street or RFD)

_____
(City)   (State)   (Zip)

_____
(Signature of church training
director)

_____
(Signature of state convention
Church Training secretary)

_____
(Date verified)

Program Planning,
Leadership Training, and Church Program
Launching Plan

THIS PLAN is designed to provide guidance for churches in the annual process of preparing for the new church year. Detailed suggestions may be found in the *Church Planning Guide*. The plan, in outline, is as follows:

Suggested Time	Church Activity	Association Activity
March	1. Elect church council	
April	2. Train church council (1) Through study (either individual or group) of *Working Together Through the Church Council* and *A Dynamic Church* (Led by pastor, minister of education, or director of church training) (2) Through summary work and discussion meeting(s)	
May	3. Begin church planning (1) Through a group study of the *Church Development Planbook* and church council study of the *Church Planning Guide* (See leadership suggestions in 2) (2) Detail the church planning process based on needs and previous planning experience.	1. *Associational Planning and Training Event for Church Council Members* sponsored by the associational church training organization and supported by all organizations of the association. This event should feature a two-hour training session for

136

LAUNCHING PLAN—Continued

church council members. It will relate to denominational emphases, goals actions, etc. Its purpose is to equip participants for local church planning.

May

4. Elect church organizational councils

May

5. Train organizational councils through individual or group studies of program manuals and related materials. Training led by organizational elected head or church staff member.

June

6. Begin organizational planning

June

7. Elect organizational workers and church officers and committees

June

8. Train organizational workers
    (1) Through organizational age-group studies led by organizational council members or other leadership especially selected for this purpose
    (2) Through studies of program and curriculum guides across church program organizational lines
    (3) Through individual study and/or scheduled group discussion-planning sessions

2. Through associational age-group central schools

July

9. Begin unit planning (class, training group, mission action group, music group, etc.)

LAUNCHING PLAN—Continued

Sept.   10. Launch church program
The Sunday School will lead in the planning and promotion of launching week and month. The Sunday School Director will work with the leaders of other church programs and services in outlining plans and activities. Launching month and week will be promoted as an annual church activity designed to communicate information about organizational and church-wide goals and plans. Emphasis will be on corporate fellowship and commitment to and through the work of the local church. Installation and recognition services for leaders will be a part of this emphasis. It is suggested that churches set aside a Sunday evening service for this purpose.

3. *Associational Launching Night* sponsored by the Associational Sunday School organization and supported by all organizations of the association.
Launching night will emphasize the importance of *program launching*. It will be designed to project the church program organizational plans. It will set forth significant denominational emphases and suggested church goals.